# The Future of Strategy

# The Future of Strategy

Colin S. Gray

polity

The right of Colin S. Gray to be identified as Author of this Work has been asserted in accordance with the UK Copyright, Designs and Patents Act 1988.

First published in 2015 by Polity Press
Reprinted 2016, 2017 (twice), 2018, 2020, 2022 (twice)

Polity Press
65 Bridge Street
Cambridge CB2 1UR, UK

Polity Press
350 Main Street
Malden, MA 02148, USA

ISBN-13: 978-0-7456-8793-3
ISBN-13: 978-0-7456-8794-0 (pb)

A catalogue record for this book is available from the British Library.

Library of Congress Cataloging-in-Publication Data

Gray, Colin S.
  The future of strategy / Colin Gray.
    pages cm
  Includes bibliographical references and index.
  ISBN 978-0-7456-8793-3 (hardback) – ISBN 978-0-7456-8794-0
(paperback)  1. Strategy.  2. War (Philosophy)  3. Nuclear
warfare–Prevention.  4. Geopolitics.  I. Title.
  U162.G692 2015
  355.02–dc23

                                                          2015003035

Typeset in 11 on 13 pt Sabon
by Toppan Best-set Premedia Limited
Printed and bound in the UK by CPI Group (UK) Ltd, Croydon

The publisher has used its best endeavours to ensure that the URLs for external websites referred to in this book are correct and active at the time of going to press. However, the publisher has no responsibility for the websites and can make no guarantee that a site will remain live or that the content is or will remain appropriate.

Every effort has been made to trace all copyright holders, but if any have been inadvertently overlooked the publisher will be pleased to include any necessary credits in any subsequent reprint or edition.

For further information on Polity, visit our website: politybooks.com

To the respected memory of
Aleksandr A. Svechin (1878–1938)
– the Russian Clausewitz

'Rules are inappropriate in strategy.'

Svechin, *Strategy*, 2nd edn (1927; Minneapolis, MIN: East View Information Services, 1992), 64

# Contents

# Preface

I am most grateful to my editor and her team at Polity Press, Dr Louise Knight, who persisted in challenging me to write relatively briefly and intelligibly. Relative brevity I did achieve, but final judgement as to intelligibility I must defer to readers. I confess that I was somewhat surprised by my own argument, and conclusions, in this book. Specifically, although I have always been sure that strategy had a secure future in our history, I had not realized, prior to writing this text, just how overwhelmingly strong the argument for strategy in our human future has to be. Readers will discover that, although my subject here is forbiddingly diverse in historical detail, the true essentials of my argument about the future of strategy are actually quite simple and intellectually cohesive. I find that our human nature demands that we organize for security, which means that we require political process and need strategy. The logic is tight and the historical evidence in its support is overwhelming. Equally, the need for strategy is certain to be as strong in the future as it has been in the past and is in the present. The argument is clear and utterly compelling, once one has worked it out. I can thank Polity for obliging me to understand and explain the future of my subject.

In addition to the staff at Polity, I must thank my professional manuscript preparer, Barbara Watts, and my wife and daughter, Valerie and Tonia, for making it possible for me to complete this challenging project.

Colin S. Gray
Wokingham

# Introduction

I am a strategist. For fifty years I have spoken, written and sought to advise governments about strategy. Because this is a relatively short book on what can be a large and often apparently diverse subject, it is necessary to start by bringing order to what otherwise can appear unduly chaotic.[1] The concept of chaos, meaning disorder and confusion, is important for our subject. Chaos always is either actively present in strategic history, or, at the least, ready in the wings threatening to become dominant in a current context. The discipline of strategy substantially is about attempts to prevent political urges from resulting in threats and violence that are not highly relevant to the motives for action. The core challenge of strategy is the attempt to control action so that it has the political effect desired. Indeed, strategy is all about the consequences of action that is tactical behaviour.

The beginning of wisdom for an approach to the understanding of strategy should be recognition of the sheer difficulty of the enterprise.[2] The challenges to the strategist are formidable wherever one looks. Scholars' text books are almost bound to simplify in the interests of clarity, but the attempted practice of strategy meets resistance that often was unanticipated, and finds itself committed largely to the prevention of chaos. However, although 'chaos rules' more often in strategic history than one might like, fortunately it is possible to identify a handful of ideas that can be helpful in making an effort to make this vitally important subject more intelligible.

## General Theory

First and foremost, the entire, hugely diverse, strategic history of Mankind has been commanded fundamentally by the dicta of a general theory of strategy that applies to all times, places and circumstances. This general theory does what such a theory must, it explains the nature and basic functioning of its subject, without privilege or prejudice to particular issues. My personal preference for a general theory of strategy contains twenty-three items at present (see table 3.1). A secure grasp of this theory serves as education that should enable practising strategists to cope better with the specific challenges they face. I developed this version of theory in the course of my professional career as the result of a pressing need to understand how best to apply military force of many kinds in action or as threats. I have found this general theory suitable as an important aid for coping with challenges regarding arms control, nuclear weapons, landpower, seapower, airpower, cyber power, special operations and geopolitics. This theory, or variants of it, has to be the essential basis for the understanding of all strategic topics.

## Politics

As the general theory brings order to all aspects of the broad subject of strategy, so too does explicit recognition of the authority of politics. Strategy is not politics, but it is always about politics. No matter the particular technical and cultural detail, strategy has to be ruled by superior political process. This is not discretionary. Violence, organized or other, always and everywhere has some political meaning. The outcome of warfare often is not what many people expected, but that does not negate the merit in this second theme. Journalists and scholars are apt to forget politics in the excitement or perceived impressiveness of policy and policymaking. But the making of policy is controlled by politics. Moreover, the dignity within which policy is wrapped can serve unhelpfully to bury from view appreciation of the politics that rule policymaking process.

## Prudence

I must emphasize prudence as the foremost quality that should discipline strategic behaviour. The reason for this unexciting-sounding argument is because all strategy has to be about the consequences of threat and action. The concept of prudence pertains to what lies at the very heart of what should be meant by strategy. Tactics is all about action, doing things, while strategy is about the consequences of the preceding tactical behaviour. The achievement by force of desirable and intended tasks, selected as policy goals by political process, is an exercise liable to hindrance and even failure as the result of the many difficulties that may assail even the competent strategist. Of all the 'laws' that often seem to harness the strategist, the law of unintended consequences is probably the one most often cited. Surprises happen, especially to the overconfident strategist! Of course, it is one thing to praise the virtue of prudence, but it can be quite another to practise it. How prudent can one be when there is no way to know what the future will bring? The future is not foreseeable, regardless of the promises of gullible or devious politicians and of ambitious generals.

## Legitimacy and Justice

This book does not shrink from recognizing the repeated realities of the grimmer aspects to strategic history, but the argument here is distinctly friendly to the linked concepts of legitimacy and justice. Of course the precise meaning of these high-sounding words varies considerably with context, but nonetheless they have universal relevance to our enduring political story. Contrary to the argument advanced by adherents to an 'offensive realist' persuasion, it is my belief that, although great powers can never afford to be indifferent to apparently adverse trends in a balance of power, neither are they condemned to seek hegemonic superiority and domination.[3] In strategic matters, as in many others, sound argument tends to become dangerously unsound when it is taken too far. It is only prudent to be somewhat conservative over issues of national security, but it can be imprudent to demonize current state antagonists when there is little convincing evidence of serious misbehaviour. This is not to condone, let alone by implication tolerate state misbehaviour that, if unopposed, is almost certain to create an imbalance of power injurious to reasonable understanding of the requirements of world order. Strategists cannot afford the luxury of primary devotion to ideals of legitimacy and justice, if necessary, at the expense of an imbalance in military power. That said, it is essential that strategists should not become so fascinated with calculations of relative military muscle that they fail to understand the potency of moral beliefs about legitimate governance and just behaviour.

## Historical Context

Readers need to be alert to the importance attached here to the idea of historical context. Although my first-hand experience in analysing strategic issues has been contemporary, often even future looking, my view of the subject of strategy is a timeless one. What this means is that I have grappled long and hard with this topic of temporal context, and with arguments about the relationship between change and continuity in history.[4] To avoid getting ahead of myself, I will confine my argument here to affirmation of belief in the essential unity of my subject. That subject is strategy and I believe it should be regarded as thought and action in a great stream of time, with no discernible beginning and no predictable conclusion. A principal challenge in regard to this belief is the need to identify plausibly, and distinguish between, what changes over time and what does not. The benefit to belief in the unity of strategic experience through all of history is that it has to mean that all historical strategic experience comprises potential evidence about the same subject. While seeking to avoid anachronism, this means that one should be able to consider strategic behaviour of all kinds in the light shed by a reasonably consistent functional view.[5] Historical context has altered dramatically as a consequence of both revolutionary and cumulative change. But, in functional terms, Greek and then Roman needs for security, and the manner in which those needs were or were not met, can be viewed in the light shed by a general theory of strategy. Such a theory is as able to cope with oar-rowed galleys and lethally pointed *gladii* as it is with the precision conventional and nuclear weapons of today. I believe that strategy can and should be studied as an inclusively united theme running through all of history.

## Motives

Finally, the view of the motives for the subject of strategy underlying this discussion is, I confess, heavily indebted to that of the great history of the Peloponnesian War by Thucydides. Suffice it to say for now that motivations for the strategic theme throughout the course of history have been summarized most persuasively by the great Athenian historian in a justly famous triptych: 'fear, honour, and interest'.[6] Due consideration of the meaning and possible implications of Thucydides' three lethal baskets of motives serves well to explain why our history has always been strategic.

The plan of campaign here opens necessarily with argument about, and explanation of the inalienable nexus between, strategy and politics, with the latter rightly always in occupation of the driving seat (chapter 1). In the analysis and argument that follow the heavily political theme of the opening chapter, I explain just what strategy is and why it matters so crucially (chapter 2); how and why strategy works in practice, if not always in theory (chapter 3); what changes as opposed to what most typically persists with strategy (chapter 4); how the general theory of strategy can be relevant even as new strategies are needed to fit new kinds of weapons and circumstances (chapter 5); and finally what all of this should mean for the future (chapter 6).

# – 1 –

# Politics the Master

## The Argument: Basics of Strategy as Enduring Narrative

In this opening chapter I explain the meaning of strategy, and in particular why and how it is connected so umbilically to our human nature and also to our practice of political behaviour. While there are other ways in which we need to contextualize strategy, by far the most important are those flagged here in this chapter. We devise and have strategy because of our human needs – most especially for security – and strategy has to be made, and to a degree executed, in a process that is always political in its nature. This is the triptych that lies at the heart of this book and runs as a master theme throughout.

Strategy can be about many things, but primarily it must always be about politics. The reason for this is that politics provides the enabling mechanism for community action. It is true that politics can take a wide array of forms, often clearly different from each other. However, with regard to the enabling of strategy, which has to be a political process, almost any such fulfils the same essential purpose. This process, whatever its local colour, confers legitimacy of authority on some executive body, which allows that body to decide, and perhaps act, on behalf of a whole political community. My aim here is to explain the nature of strategy, particularly in the context of its ever-shifting character. The more obvious changes to strategic phenomena have been so great that it is scarcely surprising that misunderstanding and even confusion have been rife. The history of strategy – or strategic history, a term I prefer – is amply littered with misconceptions, most of which are readily avoidable and indeed correctable.

Strategy in a more or less military context has been a permanent feature of human experience. This well-evidenced claim is key to understanding most aspects of our subject. We do strategy very much because we have no prudent alternative. We may do it poorly, but that is another matter. To be blunt, we do strategy because our human political condition demands it. Our human condition, more generally, also commands that we do politics. My argument comprises the austere dual claims that historical experience has allowed us no prudent choice other than to behave both politically and strategically. Recurrent controversy about Strategic Studies, or the relevance of strategy in the future, betrays a failure to comprehend the enduring human condition. Often, students considering the study of politics are confronted with the need to choose among a competing array of options. All too infrequently is it explained to them that strategy in its military connection, rather grim and old-fashioned as it may appear, is not merely an optional extra for politics. Contrary to appearances perhaps, this book is not written in any important sense to advocate for Strategic Studies. When explained properly, the case for the study of strategy all but makes itself.[1]

While we cannot know specific details about the exact character of the future, we are well informed about its recurring features, thanks to our access to our strategic history.[2] The details of this will often be uncertain or contested, but still it is possible to be reasonably sure what happened and why. It may seem contradictory to argue in the same breath that we can find evidence of change which was sometimes very rapid, and yet that little of lasting significance alters. The proposition that strategy has stayed the same across time is crucial for understanding my argument. Strategy is an eternal and ubiquitous subject.[3] This rather elementary, though imperial, idea meets some popular resistance from people who are persuaded that, because time moves on, so must the important elements in its manifestation. But the function of strategy is not necessarily to understand the contemporary realities of strategic choice, which shifts to reflect the pressures and needs of particular circumstances, times and personalities. In this book I draw a sharp distinction between the idea of strategy – singular, expressed in one general theory applicable to all historical times, places and circumstances – and strategies in the plural. The latter are the choices made by particular historical people and institutions, given the assets available to them at the time and the unique desiderata of their contexts. The biggest challenge is to be able to cope with the superficially contrasting evidence of both change and historical continuity. What unites Pericles of Athens, Julius Caesar, Edward I (and III), Moltke the Elder and the Younger, Field Marshal Sir Douglas Haig and Generals George C. Marshall, Dwight D. Eisenhower and David Petraeus is the fact that all attempted to practise strategy – though naturally within the scope of the material and ideational cultures of their day. They all needed and sought to be strategists.

A few professional historians challenge the idea advanced here that strategy is effectively an eternal necessity for prudent human behaviour. Instead, they claim that our contemporary idea of strategy can be dated only to the 1770s. This is probably true. Our modern understanding, and indeed use, of the term 'strategy' assuredly dates only to 1771.[4] However, the idea that history was devoid of attempts at strategic thought and practice prior to the late eighteenth century is absurd.[5] Our whole human history is a protracted strategic narrative, regardless of what it was called and how it was defined at the time. What is more, even when the meaning of a fairly novel concept (as in the nineteenth century when strategy focused on battle and its consequences) shifts noticeably, as strategy moved in its meaning towards policy, it is essential not to forget what did not and could not shift.[6] Functional strategists in the past could speak in Greek, Latin, French, German or whatever, and certainly were ordered in thought and behaviour by the needs of their contemporary historical contexts. But strategy is and has always been a function whose essential logic is resistant to the vagaries of particular times and places. This enduring logic holds that strategy is all about the attempted achievement of desired political ENDS, through the choice of suitable strategic WAYS, employing largely the military MEANS then available or accessible. To this fundamental triptych of ends, ways and means, it is advisable to insist upon adding the vital ingredient of ASSUMPTIONS. This fourth element is always important and typically reigns unchallenged as the greatest source of mischief for entire strategic enterprises. At least, this has been my personal experience in strategic argument conducted over five decades.

Nothing is more important than recognition of the essential Trinitarian logical nature of the interdependent strategy function. The elementary, indeed the elemental, strategic logic of the mutual dependencies of ends, ways and means (never forgetting assumptions) united functioning strategists across millennia and cultures. Problems in contemporary strategy are ever changing, but they all have common roots. It has been an eternal human strategic reality that desired political ends can only be pursued in accessible ways and by means that are mobilizable. Even though strategists and those they sought to advise have been capable of adopting almost awesomely improbable assumptions, the game has always had to be about ends,

ways, and means – though ends, meaning desired consequences, are not independently sovereign. With the possible exception of nuclear realities after 1945, it is not
possible to explain our human (strategic) history except
with reference to the strategy function, even though it has
frequently been misunderstood by contemporaries who let
their political ambitions and desires drive their assumptions down a rose-strewn path.

I should probably restate what some readers might have
found difficult to accept. I am arguing that strategy has
not changed as a broad function through the ages, and
indeed that it could not do so given the material and ideational actualities within which it is bound. Of course,
polities and their leaders can and do make mistakes – it is
often less than obvious just what contemporary ways and
means can accomplish. However, there is a discipline about
the strategy function that is literally beyond cultural influence. Cunning plans and good fortune can certainly deliver
success despite the odds calculated from a simple assessment of relative combat strengths, but plans that depend
upon enemy folly and luck have a way of ending in frustration, or much worse (e.g. Stalingrad, 1942–3, or Dien Bien
Phu, 1954).

## Roots of Strategy: Human Nature and Politics

Of course the details of change in strategic history can be
highly significant, in the space of only a generation (which
is to say twenty or thirty years). Nothing in this text denies
evidence of change in character of detail. However, change
– usually movement – is much easier to spot than continuity, with the inevitable consequence that the latter often
escapes due notice. This is unfortunate for understanding
of the meaning of the past for the present and future. It
can be quite a challenge to explain persuasively why there

is an enduring sense in past strategic choices that are relevant to the subject of strategy in history. While the past is done and gone, along with many of its consequences, the contemporary strategist needs the ability to understand the past in terms of an historical context that is still unrolling in detail. The Romans will not invade Britannia again, but the reasons why first Julius Caesar, then Emperor Claudius, did so in the first century BC continue to be relevant to strategy and its politics in the twenty-first century. In order to justify this bold claim, it is important to recognize the key elements of the argument, and the evidence needed to support them. The proposition that strategy is a timeless feature in human history can be summed up in three closely linked claims that can be fairly easily proved. The argument has the following mutually supporting constituent parts, which need to be considered as a whole.

1. *Human nature*  Despite changes in culture and circumstances, human beings both as individuals and in society have revealed a common nature in the characteristics they are able to detect or surmise across boundaries of time and place.[7] We have no difficulty understanding Herodotus and Thucydides, even though they were writing nearly 2,500 years ago. The latter historian speaks eloquently and persuasively to the political and strategic challenges of the twenty-first century.[8] Regardless of the material and cultural differences between Ancient Greece and today, these historians were plainly writing about people subject to many of the same pressures we face today and our successors will probably face in the future.

2. *Politics*  The people who are the necessary subjects in both Thucydides' great history of the Peloponnesian War and the plans and anxieties of our contemporary strategists have had no prudent choice other than to engage in political behaviour.[9] Because our human

nature has been governed by anxieties that Thucydides summarized economically in the three inclusive concepts of 'fear, honour and interest', mutual protection has had to be the defining purpose behind the ways pursued in order to secure and protect orderly governance.[10] Our human political forms have varied widely, but they have all shared the overriding purpose of providing greater human security. Political thought and behaviour – and their consequential strategic derivatives – have been permanent features in human history – often poorly done, but inevitably attempted.

3. *Strategy* If it is but human to be political, the same applies to being strategic (or at least trying to be). The need for strategy flows from the essentially competitive condition of all human life. While theory and practice have varied considerably with culture and other contexts, it is scarcely possible for a necessarily political human security community to avoid the stark logic of strategy.[11] Human communities can strive to ignore the meaning of strategic logic, but there is close to being an Iron Law of strategy that will impose discipline. Policy, which is to say political, ends sought incompetently in unsuitable ways using inappropriate (military) means will generally fail. Extraordinary good luck or the enemy's incompetence may save the 'home' side from the defeat merited by its own strategic errors, but this can never be taken for granted.[12] For present purposes, what matters most is acknowledgement of the disciplinary authority of the logic of the basic theory of strategy across time and space. No matter how contemporaries conceive of their strategic tasks, the interdependence of ends, ways and means cannot be denied and defied without repercussions. Neither Pericles nor Julius Caesar attended a Staff College, and neither of them spoke or wrote about strategy as strategists do today, but both behaved strategically. Their human political circumstances gave them no sensible alternative. Quite

often, the prudent-seeming estimates, calculations and plain guesses of statesmen and strategists will appear sufficiently well founded in the interlocking dependencies of ends, ways and means, only for the course of strategic history to demonstrate the potential for unexpected disaster. It is one thing to grasp well the bare logic of ends, ways and means, but it can be quite another to translate that grasp into an effective grip on the course of history. The historical record is amply populated with losers, not excluding those who fooled themselves into believing that there was no difference between what they believed to be possible, and what actually was. Overconfident expectation of the triumph of one's own will has been a recurring feature in strategic history. Faulty assumptions are the most deadly source of strategic error: one need look no further into the past than to the 1940s, when Nazi Germany demonstrated for all times why political ends need to be effected by suitable ways and means; or to the American experience in Vietnam in the 1960s, and then, a generation later, to the failure in Afghanistan in the 2000s.

It is both usual and probably necessary for historians to emphasize the features of their chosen historical subject that were unique to the period in question. Of course, the unfamiliar may need explanation. But, although we understand that cultures have differed in their ideas quite dramatically over time and space, it is still challenging to take at anything like face value the alien-seeming assumptions of other times. Some degree of harmful 'presentism' and parochialism appears unavoidable. We humans are self-centred and seem unable or unwilling to release what we may find in the past about the past for honest and fair appraisal. Whether or not a person is willing to accept the implications of the idea of the stream of time, all historical judgements are influenced by our placement and interpretation of them in the dynamic landscape of the past. It is impossible to resist passing historical judgement based on our privileged knowledge of what followed from the often distant events we study. An especially clear example of this phenomenon is the continuing inability of competent scholars to make thoroughly persuasive sense of an historical event as major and relatively recent as the First World War. It appears impossible to allow attitudes towards that war not to be overshadowed by our knowledge of the consequences (if they were!) for the remainder of the twentieth century. Whatever one's belief concerning the potency of continuity in history, practical recognition of the power of consequences, even if they often cannot be traced with certainty, means that it can be difficult to isolate the local sources of thought and behaviour from their earlier contextual roots. It has to follow that a study such as this needs to be able to draw a line separating lasting factors from passing ones. At the risk of admitting to a potentially confusing fuzziness, we are obliged to recognize in this study of strategy that, while there is some change in continuity, there is even more continuity accommodated well enough in change. Moreover, we believe there is a considerable asymmetry between the forces of change and those of continuity, with the latter hugely outweighing the former. When King Archidamus of Sparta addressed an assembly-conference in Sparta on the eve of the great Peloponnesian War in 431 BC, the details of his reasoning were of course historically very particular.[13] However, the King spoke with strategic reason in terms that make sense quite readily to us today, with little need for contextual translation. Even the aggressive imperial land-grabbers of the Rome of the first two centuries of the Christian era can readily be explained with reference to a standard array of state reasoning combined with personal motives, pertaining to gold, glory and fear. The leading elements fit easily enough into an enduring trans-historical explanation of high and low official motivation in a way that may be elevated unduly by the concept of statecraft for strategy.

From the Ancient Greeks to today, it proves possible, indeed is compelling, to abstract in general terms what moves political communities to act. The terse judgement in Thucydides – fear, honour and interest – has yet to be bettered. This famous triptych combines a wonderful inclusivity and adaptability with remarkable economy and clarity. The particular meaning of each of the three categories of motive needs to be allowed to be whatever it has to be to fit with local culture, because a general theory requires no more detail than is offered in Thucydides' terse prose. What matters is the fit of the triptych with the empirical evidence particular to each time, place and culture. To understand the future of strategy, it is not necessary, and probably is not even desirable, to secure a grip upon the motives – evident and presumed – of other state players in international politics. It is sufficient to know that every political community is and will be motivated by its own fears, its own sense of honour, and its own view of its interests. No matter what theory of statecraft and strategy one uses in historical explanation, I suggest that there is on offer literally no compelling alternative to Thucydides.

If Thucydides is right, the implications are profound for the future of strategy. After all, this master historian from the Ancient Greek world has captured conceptually the persisting political nature of human existence. If the need for strategy must follow inexorably from the politics that endlessly make and remake the notorious triptych, the intellectual consequence ought to be that we are well prepared for a political context that has an acute need for strategy.

## The Meaning of Politics for Policy and Strategy

Some terms are so familiar that they escape close scrutiny; politics is one. In my own writing over the years, I have tried to avoid using the term policy, and instead to privilege the concept of politics. The reason for this preference is my appreciation of the pervasive and typically determinative authority of political process. This recognition means we need an unambiguous meaning for the concept of politics. I discovered that definitions of politics tend to be confused and uncertain, despite the popularity of the term. Stripped bare to its essential functioning, politics can and should be seen as the process that produces influence over others. Political process of any and every conceivable kind is designed to generate legitimate authority in relative influence.[14] Policy, or the ends that a community strives to achieve, is the result of the contention and negotiation that are political process.[15] Those people who are most influential over opinion on particular issues are those who make policy. The sundry purposes in policy on any and every subject are the product of a struggle for relative influence.

In striving to be influential, would-be political leaders must appeal to a variety of the constituencies that serve to legitimize political authority. Because of our human nature, we are everywhere self-organized by political and often strategic effort into more or less exclusive political tribes. Of course, politicians will argue about issues and whatever has influence-conferring value in a particular political process. But one must be careful not to find substance in political process per se that is not really there. The most telling discipline by far in political process is that seen to flow from relative influence by legitimating constituencies. There is nothing in politics and political process that necessarily – let alone reliably – provides vital discipline over policy choice. It can, and probably should, be a chilling realization that the future of strategy in the twenty-first century will rest very much in people's hands, minds and emotions, much as it did in the 1910s and 1930s. History's continuity suggests an appalling open basket of grim possibilities. It is necessary to flag this openness to misfortune in policy, or political, possibilities, because the concept of policy – sometimes of politics itself – is often discussed almost reverentially. The pretentious ambition signalled by the pseudo-scientific idea of policy science should not mislead us. There are no safeguards provided by nature against employment of thoroughly inappropriate concepts by communities who are self-harming, apparently wilfully, but actually without realizing it. Only very rarely can public policy approach the condition of science, in the sense of being verifiably accurate.

The terms politics and political can be employed in an attempt to justify just about anything. It may seem unreasonably cynical to say this, but the prime duty of leading politicians in practice is to guard the high worth of their own influence. After all, if popular support is compromised, they will be unable to make and carry out the policy they need in order to gain or retain the popular approval that legitimates their authority. The 'what' of policy is always decided by the 'who' produced by political process: in other words, political process is always trumps. This persisting fact about the human condition can be explained more or less bluntly, but its unavoidable truth means that there is a shortage of safety catches on the policy – which is to say the political – behaviour of states. Any study of the future of strategy needs to retain an unblinkered grasp on this reality.

There are excellent reasons why prudence should be the primary virtue in the policy known as statecraft.[16] Prudence, meaning a particular care for the possible consequences of policy, should be the dominant principle exerting control over decision makers. However, because policymaking is an art and not a science, because it is decided and performed by flawed human beings, and because the consequences of behaviour are often unforeseen, folly (and bad luck) deservedly enjoys at least as substantial a place in the exploration of our history as does prudence. The future is not foreseeable, regardless of the popularity of the overoptimistic phrase that says otherwise.[17] Although both politics and strategy are activities variably, but still often usefully, structured to reduce the risks of imprudence, strategic history clearly records the persistence of lethal error. This is committed even by those motivated to the highest degree by considerations that should encourage prudence: concern for their personal career, even life itself, and knowledge of the possibly appalling consequences of irrecoverable policy or strategic error.[18]

Students of strategic history need to accept two typically unwelcome revelations about the politics of policymaking. First, the politics that usually determines policy is necessarily constructed by the all too human people who dominate institutions. Unsurprisingly, it is common for individuals who have extraordinary positive abilities also to be limited in their overall effectiveness in office by no less extraordinary, though unfortunate, personality traits. This trans-cultural general truth has been flagged most persuasively in – to name just one example – a powerful and highly critical recent book, pointedly titled *British Generals in Blair's Wars*.[19] The second point that applies to all human policy and strategic choice is the absence of reliable ethical filtering and auditing.[20] Of course, policymakers typically believe that they are functioning rationally, effectively connecting their political ends with their enabling ways and means. However, the unknowability of the future means that objectively reliable testing for prudence in policy and strategy literally is not possible. It follows that even rational policymaking is commonly revealed to have been founded upon unreasonable assumptions. In practice there is no ethical audit on decisions and behaviour that can be pregnant with hazardous consequences. No matter what we think will control official choice on policy and strategy, in reality 'necessity knows no law', to quote the German Chancellor Theobald von Bethmann-Hollweg from his speech to the Reichstag on 4 August 1914, aimed mainly at justifying the invasion of neutral Belgium.[21]

## Strategy: The Great Enabler

Strategy all too often defies easy portrayal, a fact that has contributed to the vagueness, ambiguity and downright error that often occur when this ominously heavy-sounding concept is involved. But, when pretension is left behind and clear direct meaning intended, this mysterious concept has vital distinctive meaning that can be stated simply. Basically, strategy enables a person, institution or state to connect its political purposes with the means that can reasonably be made available. Strategy enables a political community, or state, to use its (military) assets in the service of its policy wishes. It is the great enabler that allows tactical combat power to be translated into desirable consequences; this is called strategic effect.[22] An army is an inventory of military possibilities that cannot itself decide what or how much action to attempt. There can be no magical wisdom lurking inherently in strategy itself, the idea or the institutions to effect it, but sound strategic method enhances the prospects for success in achieving a productive marriage between ends and means.

Definitions are critically important if we are to agree on what it is that we are discussing. I offer three definitions of strategy: one of which, by Lawrence Freedman, I dislike; one by the intellectual father of this subject, Carl von Clausewitz; and then my own preference, which is unapologetically Clausewitzian. Bearing in mind that definition should aid clear understanding in explaining its subject, and ought not to advance a particular – possibly controversial – point of view about it, I decline to endorse Freedman's choice of the following. He argues that 'strategy is the central political art. It is about getting more out of a situation than the starting balance of power would suggest. It is the art of creating power.'[23] For me, this definition is not so much wrong as inappropriate and overloaded with inference. By way of no little contrast, Clausewitz advises repeatedly that 'Strategy is the use of the engagement for the purpose of the war.'[24] My choice of definition, dominant in these pages, is 'Military strategy is the direction and use made of force and the threat of force for the purposes of policy as decided by politics.'[25] This is a little cumbersome, but it clarifies the master role of politics in the whole strategy production process, which is critically important to understanding. As Freedman explains, and as Beatrice Heuser illustrates in meticulous historical detail, the meaning of what today is called strategy has migrated considerably both within and between languages and generally in the direction of politics and policy rather than tactics.[26] In my preferred metaphorical terms, strategy should serve as a bridge between military power and political purpose; it can and should be the great enabler.

Time after time in this book it will be necessary to distinguish between continuity and change – in the form, first, of strategy in the single enduring sense of general theory, and, second, of strategies, plural, meaning the ways that historical figures have found to employ the military means of their day. People have always attempted to succeed with strategy, even though frequently they have not done so: it is extremely hard to perform competently as a strategist, not least because circumstances often won't let you. Think of Germany in 1944–5, or of any events likely to lead to all-out nuclear war.[27] Strategy always requires the translation of the dicta from general theory into the relevant specifics required for contemporary practice. While the general theory should assist competent practice, virtually every challenge in strategic history has contained a need for some particular application of then contemporary military prowess. The general theory can evolve in the kind of understanding it can confer, but our ambition is for it to serve as the repository of timeless wisdom. This is why no Ancient Greek wisdom on strategy, no matter how prudently conceived and tested, can contribute usefully to our understanding unless it can rise above a technological context based on oared galleys and close-quarter hoplite phalanx battle. Arguably, analogies may well be imagined that claim to connect then with now. As a rule, each technological era must and will devise its own strategies that fit with its own unique changing circumstances. However, assuming that our general theory of strategy is amended prudently, there will always be a masterful set of explanations about how strategy can and should function: this is the key indispensable role of the general theory. At the very least it should rule out overenthusiastic adoption of wisdom that will become outdated in the relatively near term. Time and again, during the past century, excited advocates of military novelty have expressed unwonted faith in the ability of their favourite new 'toys' to upset the apple cart of established strategic truth. To date, with the possible striking exception of nuclear weapons, such claims have been neither verified nor even found persuasive for very long. Contemporary consideration of the promise in cyberpower should benefit from this longer-term view.

Returning to the theme of continuity and change, the attempted practice of strategy will be as near continuous as it must be endless. Particular problems may well be resolved, or simply endured (as will Israeli problems with the Palestinian Arabs, and vice versa) but there will always be a need for strategy, though the relative significance of the shifting political ends, chosen strategic ways and available means – military and other – may alter over time. The human race is condemned permanently to need and therefore to seek governance, which means that it is obliged to behave politically, and it cannot avoid endlessly trying to function strategically. There can be no end to this human condition, apart from the grossly unpleasant possibility of a self-harming nuclear catastrophe. It is in the interest of reducing the risk of such an end to our strategic history that one writes books such as this one.

# – 2 –

# Strategy: What It Is, and Why It Matters

Strategy should be thought of as glue that holds together the purposeful activities of state. It is the great enabler, as I explained at the close of chapter 1. Strategy interconnects all of the different behaviours and capabilities that a security community commands. Expressed tersely, strategy provides the 'how' answer to what in its absence are political ambition and military activity, with each effectively isolated. Strategy can be considered a system that enables functional cooperation among categorically distinctive behaviours in the interest of advancing some common purpose. Strategy only has value when it serves as a bridge between purpose and action. All political communities have policy preferences and goals; these are defined by political process. Also, all communities command human, mechanical, and electronic assets that are capable of doing things. But those communities do not need armed forces that can simply 'do stuff'! What every community needs are ideas and plans that carry some plausible promise of enabling the political means of military capability to resist or apply the threat of violence. This is the vital role of strategy; it answers explicitly the 'how' question that state policy may well have neglected.

In this chapter, I take an unblinkered look at how strategy should work, while also recognizing that often the strategy system collapses in the mud and blood of failure. Readers need to appreciate that although strategy can sound friendly and even rather simple to do, in practice it is menaced by incompetence, enemies with superior cunning, and sheer accident. There is always a great deal that can go wrong with strategy.

## The Bridge

The idea of strategy has been exposed clearly in major European languages since the 1770s, but its exact meaning has commonly been disputed.[1] Even today, despite the popularity of the idea, definitions of strategy are typically contested. This is not simply a matter of scholars squabbling over academic detail, because 'strategy' and 'strategic' have been adopted as working, as well as decorative, ideas employed to distinguish particular behaviour. The misuse of 'strategy' has damaging consequences for both public and official understanding. It is important to insist upon correct and consistent linguistic use of 'strategy' and 'strategic', because these ideas are essential for our security. So, what is strategy? Plainly, we are not going to be able to make much progress here unless this question can be answered in readily accessible terms. The word 'strategy' – though certainly not the idea – derives from classical Greek and pertains to leadership in the art of war. For my purposes here, I choose to retain the common military focus of the term. A problem has arisen recently due to the popularity of the word strategy, and the idea behind it. In modern English, 'strategy' and 'strategic' have attracted up-market and respectful devotees who have discovered that undisciplined employment of the idea of strategy triggers positive responses from an audience. Strategy would seem to have conquered rather indiscriminately, to the extent that everyone favours the idea: its confident deployment suggests a sense of chosen direction for an enterprise.

Although there is no correct authorized definition of strategy, it is possible to identify the most important meaning of the term. I take a functional view, which privileges the idea that strategy fulfils an essential bridging function. The 'strategy bridge' – as I see it –serves to connect purposefully a polity's military assets with its political wishes, which is to say with its policy. This should not be regarded as a – let alone as the – correct definition, but rather as one that identifies and exposes well enough what strategy is about and what it does. In metaphorical effect, strategy provides an enabling service that allows a polity to use its military power in ways likely to advance its political desires. The idea of the bridging function serves helpfully to explain what strategists need to do with strategy. Because important definitions remain unpoliced, different scholars will choose to place their preferred emphasis on their own understanding of the meaning of the concept we are examining. I would remind readers of the definition of strategy most favoured by Freedman and quoted in chapter 1 above, though not endorsed here. Freedman is not wrong, but his emphasis upon 'creating power' is not to my mind sufficiently comprehensive to justify choosing it as the standard meaning.[2] The view taken here is that strategy needs to be understood basically as the connecting and organizing function that enables a polity to pursue its goals, in the face of largely foreign competitors, with the intelligent use of its several means. Although there is no strict linguistic necessity for the concept of strategy to require military reference, that is a very common meaning and it is the one favoured for strategy in this text. Above all, this discussion of strategy's future is most concerned with exploring strategy as the most essential of bridging functions for a polity's security.

To many people, strategy is a mysterious, perhaps even sinister, phenomenon. Evidence of its authority can be clear enough as a matter of rather abstract logic, but more tangible proof of its sovereign power can be elusive. This is scarcely surprising, because the strategic function is exercised only on the operational – and above all tactical – levels. When a military operation is assessed as having had some notable strategic significance, what is meant is that there was a strategic effect caused largely by that action.[3] Whereas it is a simple matter to show photographs of military power doing a tactical job in combat, it is more than a little challenging to provide convincing proof of success in strategy. Even many supposed strategic experts are not entirely to be trusted in their grasp of just what is meant by the adjective 'strategic'. Often, you will find, the term is empty of sensible and consistent meaning. It is frequently employed simply as a heavyweight term implying relatively high importance, relating to something allegedly Big! When thus used without linguistic discipline, the concept both loses all value and hinders intelligent debate. You will find the termed misused as meaning most important, long-range or, simply, worthy of unusual attention. When confronted with such promiscuous misuse, there is no better intellectual corrective than a return to the definition quoted in chapter 1, from Carl von Clausewitz: 'Strategy is the use of the engagement for the purpose of the war.'[4] In short, strategy is all about consequences; most particularly, the consequences of military threat and action for the course of subsequent political events. It should be needless to add that the evidence for strategic gain is usually more difficult to assess than that for the acquisition of operational or tactical-level advantage.[5] All strategic success or failure has to be produced at the 'working level', as it were – in the field of actual violence applied tactically. Strategic thought may be essential, but the schemes of the strategic thinkers can only be realized in practice by actual – usually very dangerous – behaviour carried out by someone (else!). Strategy in the doing is simply tactics.

The bridging function that strategy must perform can be satisfied by a wide range of institutional possibilities, though historical experience and common sense point in favour of formal process, rather than informal arrangements of immediate convenience and perhaps temporary expediency. The challenge is to connect military power with its political purpose so that a polity's armed forces are truly working as an instrument of state policy, as Clausewitz insisted ought to be the case. The point may seem obvious, but all of strategic history serves to demonstrate the difficulty of threatening and using military power effectively and efficiently for political purposes. Although war should be regarded as an instrument of policy made by politics, mere wishing does not make it so, and never has.

The Clausewitzian dictum about military instrumentality is beyond reproach as an ideal, but in practice it frequently proves to be a bridge too far.[6] The main reason for this is easy to identify: politics and war are very different activities. Moreover, whereas policy is constructed largely, if not quite exclusively, by a domestic process of governance, war needs to be conducted against an inevitably uncooperative adversary. Although war is about politics, it is not politics, and nor is it policy by another name; many commentators and theorists fail to understand this. In fact, more often than not, war, supposedly an instrument of policy choice, seems to assume a life of its own. Whatever the political causes of hostilities, including those that persist into a period of combat, the course of the war itself will put compelling pressures on all participants. When a polity goes to war it is usually choosing to accept the verdict produced by the fighting. Policy preference may not change, but such largely pre-war choice is unlikely to survive substantially unrevised by the course of military events in the field. War, as Clausewitz insisted, is the realm of chance.[7] So greatly can its course differ from what was expected, that correction or even reversal of action is often demanded by high policy that is beyond the control of a single belligerent. Great Britain went to war on 3 September 1939 counting France and Poland as its principal allies. By early December 1941, both France and Poland had been compelled by defeat to leave the British column, to be replaced – albeit more than amply – by the Soviet Union and the United States.

In principle, there is no question as to the proper relationship between politics and war, but historically, in practice, politics is often more an instrument of war than vice versa, at least temporarily. While strategy ought to bridge what is often a completely unfordable river separating the political from the military spheres, making that work constructively for both banks – the military establishment and the society with its policy that it should protect – can be a severe challenge. In some cases, the strategy bridge simply cannot function – in fact, it may not even be permitted to exist. The most glaring (and repeated) example of the bridge not working was the case of Germany in the two world wars. Neither in 1914–18, nor in 1939–45, did Germany have a strategy-making institution capable of guiding warfare in accord with political sense. What happened was that in both wars Germans fought with great skill and determination, but fortunately they were not directed by strategy to achieve a reasonable political purpose. What was lacking, or impossible, for both Imperial and Nazi Germany was the construction and employment of a strategy bridge.

## How Strategy Works: Removing the Mystery

Strategy is an intellectual activity: it is the level of effort that orders the military behaviour that should deliver some, at least, of the consequences commanded by the political high ground of policy aims. Although the label 'strategy' is often attached to particular kinds of military power, in fact all military power has at least some potential to be strategic. It is sensible to adopt, as a principle, the view that all military behaviour has strategic meaning, be it ever so small. Strategy is about the intended consequences of that behaviour. It has to follow, in theory and in actuality, that strategy is carried out by all supposedly sub-strategic military elements.[8] These elements are often organized into both tactical units that do or support the fighting and operational-level commands (groups of units) that typically are task-focused or refocused as situations change. However, the fundamental differences in what I have just outlined are: (1) the distinction between the political purposes of the military threats or action (policy), and the sustainment and exercise in action of the armed forces that it is hoped will coerce the enemy into political compliance with our wishes; (2) the distinctions between policy purpose derived from politics, and strategy which is all about the direction and guidance of the military action intended to coerce; (3) the difference between the fighting power of a belligerent which, in the raw, is all in the realm of tactics, and an operational level of tactical behaviour, which clusters and commands tactical combat units for the purpose of generating desirable consequences beyond the view of the next hedgerow. Lest this description is not quite as clear as it needs to be, figure 2.1 offers a stripped-down guide to the bare structural essentials of our subject.

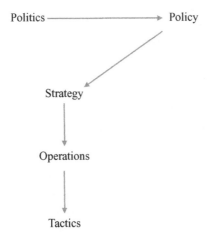

**Figure 2.1**   Strategy: elements and levels

The simple structure identified in figure 2.1 may and often does conceal truly lethal difficulties. For example, politics may not produce a clear, consistent, action-worthy policy; policy may demand too much of military strategy; and strategy can find that its tactical combat power, no matter how it is organized and reorganized into operational groupings, is unable to succeed in beating the enemy. What this all means is that, regardless of the wonderful interdependent fit of the elements in figure 2.1, the historical reality may be disastrous. Basically, strategy is inherently always menaced by the potential for poor performance from above and below in the hierarchy of authority. In practice, the strategist will almost always find himself ordered to deliver the conditions that should enable, though not inevitably, the goals of policy. The root cause of his embarrassment will often be not so much the folly of the political enterprise to which the civilian politicians have committed him and his forces as the inability of his tactical combat units to perform effectively in the field of battle.

Given the recurring historical evidence of folly in policy and of failings in troop fighting power, it may seem reasonable to question the merit in the concept of strategy. What use can it be if it is often officially obliged to attempt the politically impossible, or to triumph in combat for which it is not sufficiently well prepared (or its forces are simply too few)? Ironically, the potential shortcomings in strategic performance, far from being faults, are instead the most important prompts to improved performance.[9] The elementary conceptual structure for strategy and its context of hierarchical authority makes unmistakeably clear what needs to be done. Of course, human organization, personalities, the enemy, chance and accident must threaten to de-rail orderly, economical and efficient strategic performance, but merely to cite the obvious hazards to strategy is not to make a compelling argument. The working dynamics, the engine of strategy, comprises just four essential contributing parts. These are expressed in figure 2.2, again in starkly austere form.

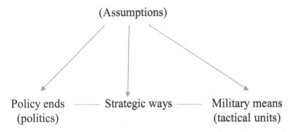

**Figure 2.2**   The fundamental architecture of strategy

In an attempt to explain what probably happened, the elementary architecture in figure 2.2 can help unravel the problems that strategy has needed to face in the conduct of every conflict in history. The particular value of this diagram is that it is a robust structure that should lead to the development of possible explanations of events, from ancient Greece in the fifth century BC, to Afghanistan in the 2000s and beyond. The logic in the diagram is unusually compelling, as well as attractively uncluttered, and it directs the reader to focus on the most critical elements in this story. For example, the grand policy objective of the Third Reich was clear enough in ambition, albeit somewhat vague in its vision of geopolitical closure, with a stable frontier roughly on a line between Archangel on the White Sea in the Arctic, down to Astrakhan on the Caspian. Germany and its Allies initially committed nearly 4 million men to an enterprise of ruthless conquest for empire building that proved beyond the combat (tactical and operational) prowess of their armed forces to deliver, given the historical context within which operational artistry had to be applied.[10] The mismatch between Germany's apparently limitless policy ends and her accessible and usable military means – no matter how well they could be organized, directed and fought – predictably proved fatal to the whole extravagant adventure in the East. The same essential elements are equally fateful when applied to explain why Germany ultimately lost the First World War in the year of decision, 1918. The particular magic in the guiding formula that is ends, ways and means – and assumptions

– lies in its value for reminding us of the most essential working parts of any human enterprise. It should be hard to misunderstand purpose, method, competence in doing – and initial beliefs that may or may not be proved by subsequent events to have been sufficiently well founded.[11]

Given that strategists have obviously failed in droves throughout all of recorded or inferable strategic history, it is plain to see that the three- (or four-) part formula above all too often has not been understood, has been respected but on the basis of false assumptions, or has simply been judged irrelevant to some particular polities' situations. There are occasions when some action in self-defence is believed to be mandatory, even though the prospects for successful resistance do not look attractively high: 'We are coming, ready or not'! States can sometimes act out of a sense of honour in a believed obligation to fight, as for a distinctly arguable historical case did Britain in 1914 with respect to its reaction to German violation of Belgium's neutrality (of which Britain appeared to be a willing guarantor).

There were apparently sound reasons for Britain to fight, related to maintaining the balance of power in Europe, but this belief was rather too abstract for enthu-siastic popular endorsement. It had been eminently pos-sible to wage limited war in the eighteenth century for the sake of the balance of power on the continent, but those days had long gone by 1914. Although all wars are more or less distinctive, with quite individual characteristics of detail and context, our understanding of how strategy works directs us to insist upon a definite answer to the critically important question, 'how'? Regardless of the issues involved, the strategist has to insist that the civilian policy–political bank to the strategy bridge provides a practicable answer to the question of purpose. The issue should not be 'Why are we considering fighting?', but rather 'What must we attempt to achieve?'. This may appear blindingly obvious, but the historical record shows time after time just how challenging it can be to settle upon satisfactory, let alone consistent, policy ends. That said, one must admit that there are times when the waging of a war currently underway is not in practice capable of producing military action that is likely to result in a satisfactory outcome. Because every war is unique in some important features, every war will have its own dynamics. Whatever the initial reasons for going to war, they are always subject to the possibility of being revised. Given that wars are sometimes waged between polities who have not fought each other before, or at least not for many years, it is hardly surprising to find a high frequency of inaccurate expectations of how well 'our troops' will fare in battle. Armed forces of all kinds are not simply interchangeable units of fighting power; their ability to deliver military advantage enabling a policy goal of strategy is often little more than paperwork founded on hope. One of the leading reasons why strategy proves so difficult to do well is that it involves the maximum number and range of factors likely to have some influence on the course of events.

The policy ends developed out of largely domestic political process may be relatively great or small; it will be the duty of the strategist to decide how much or little military force ought to suffice to produce strategic success. Most wars are conducted for limited purposes. It has been rare in strategic history for a strategist to be given the straightforward mission simply to achieve the enemy's defeat, though even in that unusual situation there will be many considerations besides the main event that is the clash of arms between the principal protagonists. For example, although the strategist will be most concerned with ensuring the competitive success of his forces waging warfare tactically and operationally, he also cannot be indifferent to the political stability of the home front – a concern included in the very high concept of grand strategy. It should never be forgotten that all foreign and defence policy is made mainly at home, and that 'home' can, and often does, pull the political plug on a strategic enterprise in which public confidence is seriously lacking. In the First World War, for example, among the principal belligerents, only in Britain was there no domestic collapse of public morale, or of the will to win. As a general rule, the armed forces of a society are not cut off from contact with circumstances at home. As a consequence of the IT revolution in social media this phenomenon is becoming ever more politically significant. Soldiers with mobile phones are very difficult to limit and control. Even in the largely pre-IT era of the protracted American combat experience in Vietnam (1965–73), the loss of domestic confidence in the wisdom of the military effort had a debilitating effect upon all aspects of the national strategy. This was an extreme example of the damage wrought by the loss of domestic support, but it does point up the need for strategy to rest upon consent on the home front.

Because the context and character of conflicts can differ so greatly, the general theory of strategy cannot possibly provide reliable useful guidance in answer to the strategist's pressing need for 'how' advice.[12] He will need to know, and will endeavour to discover, 'how to win' well enough to deliver a defeated enemy, in the circumstances of his time. Moreover, if 'his time' goes on for too long, perhaps due to military stalemate, he will have to be prepared to revisit the policy ends that he has been given or managed to forge for himself. Occasionally, radical revision is not feasible. In the twentieth century, the consequence was that the two World Wars both lasted until one side was clearly defeated. Although the First World War was halted with an armistice in the first instance, there was no serious doubt at the time that Germany had been defeated; the only question remaining was just how thoroughgoing that defeat would be allowed by victors' politics to be. After all, the defeated enemy of this war may be a necessary ally in the next one.

Although this narrative must focus primarily on the very substantial military dimension of strategy, it must also recognize the extensive domain of necessity in strategic thinking. It may be recalled from the earlier discussion that I pointed out that the logic of strategy was as mandatory for collective human behaviour, as that behaviour was obliged to be political and stimulated by Thucydides' great enduring triptych of motives: fear, honour and interest. It is simply a fact of life, public and private, that strategic thinking is obligatory for us as human beings. Most of our enterprises – political, social, moral and certainly military – call for practical application of the fundamental logic that is basically one of ends, ways, and means – resting on some current assumptions. In an extreme form, our government was confronted with the need to devise a strategic answer to the policy challenge of 'how to defeat Germany'. It is rather more common for governments to need to find out just how much defeat will need to be imposed on an enemy, in order for him to be brought to see the error of his ways (as we see it). In other words, policy ends will not usually be entirely obvious in selecting themselves. It is scarcely surprising that the political selection of policy ends is the zone of choice most liable to error and, therefore, most fatal to the prospects for success. In practice, polities find that their preferred policy ends need adjusting in the face of opposition both from abroad and at home. This importance of strategic argument obviously contributes hugely to inconsistency of strategic effort, not to mention political embarrassment (including dishonour) when high-sounding strategic ambition deflates when faced with difficulties.

## When Strategy Is Absent or Confused

In contrast to tactics, operational art and strategy are not strictly necessary qualities for the command and guidance of armed forces. When the latter are absent, soldiers can simply fight as best their tactical combat power allows and – who knows? – possibly the outcome will be significant military advantage, or the prevention of important disadvantage. Although I am emphasizing the importance of strategy, our subject here is not akin to ammunition, food and drink, or the will to resist. This is fortunate because armed forces are often committed to fight even though there is scant evidence of any grip by command authority worthy of being labelled 'strategic'. There is no thoroughly reliable – and so, verifiable – test that one can administer in order to detect the presence and content of strategy. But, accepting a lesser standard of proof, there is little practical difficulty in detecting whether any strategy exists. Just ask: 'Was there a strategy or was there not?' And, if there was, was it followed successfully? Judgements about the wisdom and skill of particular strategists have to depend upon the course of events for which they were at least partially and competitively responsible. It may be objected by some readers – not entirely unfairly – that military success on campaign and in battle usually has many more parents than simply an individual strategist's genius. For example, sheer accident, friendly *fortuna*, enemy incompetence (and bad luck), and not least the skill and combat morale of one's troops, can more than suffice to deliver campaign advantage or even success in a war generally.[13] But, although it is important not to exaggerate the potency of strategy and strategists, it is even more important that they should not be undervalued. Apparent dramatic success or failure attracts a mythology about 'master strategists' and the like.[14] The remarkable story of the rapid rise and even more rapid fall of General David Petraeus is a classic case in point. A man of high competence, he nonetheless did not and could not achieve a near miracle, in either Iraq or Afghanistan.[15] There is always a hope that there will be a 'saviour general' who can rescue an apparently forlorn effort by his individual strategic genius. Popular reasons commonly advanced for strategic failure or success rarely rise above the level of unhelpful journalism.

It should be obvious that any army committed to warfare without proper strategic guidance is likely to be at serious risk of finding its efforts and sacrifices unrewarded by military (or strategic) gains, let alone by achieving the overall political purpose. At the elevated level of national military strategy – or national security strategy, in contemporary American, and also recently British, terms – it has to be the strategy that connects the political arguments of policy with the necessary military effects, hopefully leading to a general strategic effect. One needs to ask, if the 'strategy bridge' either does not exist or is in a state of terminal disrepair, just what might serve to connect a polity's military effort with its political intentions? In nearly every war that is waged, both great and small, there will be alternative ideas on how military forces should be used, but which to choose? Imperial Japan might have been brought to defeat in any one, or a combination, of the following ways: (1) a maritime drive dominated by the US Navy, and exploiting the amphibious capabilities of the US Marine Corps, across the Central Pacific, leading, in the most important stage, to occupation of the Mariana Islands, within bombing range of the Japanese home islands; (2) an amphibious campaign through the Dutch East Indies, bringing the Philippines and Taiwan primarily under US Army command, preparatory to an invasion of Japan; (3) a long-range bombing campaign against Japan to be conducted from the mainland of China, led by the US Army Air Forces; (4) a maritime blockade of Japan's home islands to be conducted by the US Navy's submarines and, eventually, airpower – or, might the strategic mission to deliver Japan's surrender be secured by just two atomic bombs dropped by long-range aircraft very newly based in the Marianas? In actuality, the United States attempted all four of the dominant strategies just outlined. Had the atomic bombs on Hiroshima and Nagasaki not succeeded in persuading Japan to concede defeat, a primarily American invasion was definitely scheduled to follow later in 1945.

If we turn briefly from the global politics and strategy of the Second World War to the lesser challenges of the

2000s, unsurprisingly we discover yet again a pervasive and enduring absence of consistency in strategic choice. Readers are invited to pick their own preferred choice of words, but it is plausible to argue that in neither Iraq nor Afghanistan did the sizeable effort led by the United States benefit from the guidance of the eternal wisdom in the interdependent logic of the ends, ways and means of strategy. What attainable policy–political ends should have guided our military and developmental efforts? Were there any military operational level objectives that we should have pursued, for their value to the whole international endeavour? We know that American, British, Canadian and some Afghan allied forces fought hard at the tactical level in their particular parts of Afghanistan, but how did that advance the whole multi-national project of aid and direct assistance?[16] Because every polity will have its own distinct set of priorities, the making and conduct of strategy in an alliance has always been exceptionally challenging. More often than not, the most obvious consequence of an over-abundance of would-be strategy-makers has been to make such purposive activity an impossible task.

It may appear ironic to say this, but strategy still makes sense even in contexts where plainly it is largely absent or confused. The reason for making this apparently contradictory claim is because all relevant behaviour (here, primarily military) has strategic meaning, regardless of the quality of its higher direction. For example, an army that is underemployed in time of war will have a strategic consequence through its relative inactivity, even if the reasons it wasn't purposefully deployed can be traced to disagreements on the strategy bridge about its most effective use.

One needs also to be open to consideration of the importance of rather mundane pressures, as well as of ones that can be traced to superior strategic, or even operational-level, designs. Although this discussion of strategy must drag responsibility for reasoning up the chain of command, up to the strategy bridge and beyond, it is important not to forget the practical dominance of the tactical mind-set, and occasionally of the operational-level focus. That is, all armed forces operate tactically all of the time – theirs is a tactical world; the strategic realm may be more important, but it can also appear largely abstract and inherently difficult to grasp. Operations and strategy derive from a mixture of the imagination of (largely) military leaders and circumstances of danger or perceived advantageous opportunity. Strategy and an operational focus are imposed on necessarily tactical forces from outside the unavoidable realm of the conduct of 'soldiering'. If strategy and operations fail to get to grips with the tactical military forces, the latter will attempt to do what they know how to do well enough, but typically they will only act with imagination when prompted by opportunity or desperation. Soldiers live in a world of potential tactical peril most of the time when in situations of active conflict. They will not direct themselves, as if by operational or strategic autopilot, towards the attaining of strategically meaningful objectives. Operational and strategic value will vary, but all military behaviour is inherently tactical. The reality of this eternal truth is not as widely understood as it should be. There can be no necessarily strategic action, because the strategic quality only lies in the consequences of (tactical) behaviour.

Professional soldiers are committed to a world that is always of a tactical kind: it is about surviving and hopefully succeeding in the relevant battlespace on land, at sea, by air, and possibly in space, and at least about cyberspace. The physical, intellectual and, above all, the moral challenges of combat performance are overwhelmingly tactical in kind; in practice, it is not often primarily about desired consequences – at least it does not appear that way to those attempting to survive today in order to be fit enough for duty tomorrow.[17] But when strategy and operational artistry are absent or confused, the tactical consequences for troops can be appalling. Because strategy can only be done through the agency of the tactical, it has to be entirely hostage to the consequences of tactical performances, friendly and unfriendly. Whether tactical performance advances strategic designs, both grand and lesser, should not be left to be resolved by *fortuna*, and it most certainly cannot be left to the professional or instinctive wishes of narrowly military soldiers.

## Strategy: Limitations and Substitutes?

This chapter has begun to signal reasons why it would be unwise to look too expectantly towards the 'strategy bridge' in search of solutions to the more troubling problems of the day. By far the most restricting of reasons for not placing substantial faith in strategy is the sheer difficulty of the enterprise.[18] Strategy is exceedingly challenging to do well, a fact that can hardly be unexpected given that it is often required to wreak its magic in the face of competing strategic effort by a polity's adversaries inspired by each of the deadly triptych comprising fear, honour and interest. When the particular challenges to armed forces needing to be willing and able to function both tactically and consequentially to intended operational and strategic effect are fully appreciated, the scale of the problem for strategy becomes all too apparent. Nothing said in this chapter is intended to suggest that strategic behaviour can be unimportant. However, the practical challenges, particularly from tactical or operational foci that in practice cannot be made to accommodate strategic and political aims, can be lethal. Moreover, the unavoidable challenge of a potentially deadly tactical context can easily divert military effort away from achieving strategically significant goals. Tactics, operations and politics are all necessary parts of the strategist's proper context at all times, but none of them, singly or together, is able to do the connecting job that is uniquely the province of strategy.

It can be difficult to persuade a professional military audience that there are not, indeed cannot be, adequate substitutes for strategy. The same scepticism inclines soldiers to believe that there are nearly always good enough substitutes to be found for missing elements in a strategy. Experience, however, tells us that there are no such adequate substitutes, and also that the limitations upon strategy's value are as likely to be material and situationally specific as conceptual.

A significant reason why strategy is difficult to design and then execute is that its success or failure is reflected in net operational and tactical achievement. When scholars and commentators speculate as to the value of *our* strategy over *their* strategy, they are talking about the net consequences of military activity, both tactical and operational. Soldiers breathe, eat, and sleep tactics. What strategy should do, however, is provide purpose and direction to the soldiers' tactical effort.

It is appropriate to consider limitations on strategy as being in two possible categories: the first, conceptual; the second, that of combat competence. The first category refers to the differing natural gifts of strategists in their ability to imagine how best to solve particular strategic problems. The government will decide to fight, but how should the fight be conducted, and where, favouring which military instruments, and to what particular militarily achievable ends? How should NATO be defended if it is attacked? There will nearly always be apparent alternatives, and there will be advocates for each of them. The second broad category of limitations refers to the availability of a military instrument that is capable of accomplishing the goals set by the chosen strategy. Even if a country or alliance conceives of a truly brilliant strategy, will its armed forces – and also the most relevant domestic publics – prove capable of performing as necessary? There is a lasting danger that outstanding 'map strategy' will prove unduly demanding of the people who actually must perform the strategy tactically. It is important not to forget that strategy, for all its importance, always has to be done tactically by those who are more or less capable and are tolerably willing. Many popular and scholarly works on strategic history fail to cope convincingly with the key differences between strategy and tactics. This is a systemic challenge that is inadequately treated both by academia and often in the field in military practice.

# – 3 –

# Theory and Practice

Soldiers most typically are pragmatic people devoted professionally to the solving of real problems in a context that is very active as opposed to contemplative. A career dominated by the need to be pragmatically successful in the execution of orders is not one likely to be overly empathetic to the requirements of creative strategy making. Many soldiers – perhaps most – are relatively uninterested in the reasons why they are ordered to do what they do. Their professional military context is shaped and driven largely by ever-challenging 'how' questions. The purpose of this chapter is to explain why the theory of strategy matters deeply. Contrary to the rather casual opinion of some self-styled pragmatic soldiers, the principal function of strategic theory is simply explanation. As mentioned earlier in this text, strategic affairs always are, or appear to be, either chaotic or dangerously confused.

Given that military affairs can require the participation of thousands, possibly millions, of people, organized by functions in a host of organizations, in politically and culturally distinctive communities, and that they need to be directed for common strategic purposes, it is scarcely surprising that few people are able to grasp intellectually the scale of the endeavour involved. Moreover, if, or when, understanding of a strategic context is achieved, we need to remember that warfare is a game that two or more will play, and it is one that will have a different character in particular environments. In other words, two or more complex organizations of political authority (principally states) need to cooperate to some degree if they are to collaborate in waging war with each other. While theory with a restricted domain of intended authority is devised and taught to educate military specialists about their duties, also there is need for a general theory of strategy, covering all threats and uses of armed force. The importance of a general theory of strategy is explained and emphasized below.

## General Theory

As the outstanding Russian strategic thinker Aleksandr A. Svechin observed in 1927, the tradition of modern strategic thinking does not extend back in time beyond the 1770s.[1] However, Svechin was referring strictly to explicit conceptualization recognizable as such to modern strategists. He was right. Greek, Roman, Chinese and indeed Barbarian education in matters that have come to be known as strategic, did not exist. This apparent silence should not mislead us, though, because in functional terms strategy has always been a demand that human (and arguably even some non-human primates')[2] societies have been compelled to levy on those who have assumed some duty to protect their community. We cannot find explicit theories of strategy in ancient texts, but we must not be deceived by that. It is not foolishly anachronistic to detect what we would term strategic argument in the choices made by Pericles and Archidamus, though it is if we are careless and weight the factors in the controversial choices made by those city statesmen as we do today, rather than as they most probably did then.[3] The great Peloponnesian War of

431–404 BC was a protracted grand strategic struggle. The leaders of the protagonists were obliged to reason in terms that, presented to the public, would have sounded thoroughly modern and strategic (for their culture, place and time). Our access to the contemporary evidence is admittedly imperfect, but it is more than adequate for us to be certain that strategy in today's sense was practised in a period long departed. Strategy as we now understand it has been conceptualized and applied throughout history, regardless of what it was called. The notion that strategy is a relatively modern discovery that could not be used prior to its theoretical development in the last quarter of the eighteenth century, in English, French, German and Italian, needs to be slain and buried.

It is true to claim that there were no ancient texts on strategy conceived and constructed along lines that would invite comparison with the modern (post-1770s) concept. But the essential content of recent strategic theorization can be located in texts dating from the distant past, as well as in the variable evidence of deeds and misdeeds.[4] Unsurprisingly, evidence of strategic thought and behaviour is to be found in all places and periods of human history, regardless of language used or the reason for its need. Strategic thought can appear to be so closely linked to the anxieties and ambitions of particular human societies that one can fail to see what endures across time, space and context. In order to ensure that readers are not misled into overvaluation of the importance of historically specific political troubles, we need to identify what has emerged in recent times as the enduring truth about the more important elements of strategy. For convenience, we can think of these elements as forming strategy's general theory. I believe that a general theory can be quarried from the multitude of writers on the subject, and distilled in the water of historical experience.[5] What follows here is explanation of what has been found to be the persisting human practice of strategy. Typically, I have preferred to treat the separable elements of this theory as 'dicta', meaning serious formal announcements, rather than as theory. So much of the understanding and attempted practice of strategy has derived from particular anxieties and worldviews, that it is unwise to risk promoting undue excitement by claiming to have discovered the meaning and implications of strategy. However, even a prudent modesty cannot be allowed to discourage us from the major task of theorization. I do not claim that what follows as theory is reliably trustworthy for all of the strategic experience of the human race, but I do believe that table 3.1 is as correct as it can be for now, when expressed in terms designed to evade the confining realm of specific choice. 'The General Theory of Strategy' is a distillation of the wisdom of centuries – actually, millennia – as expressed by the pens of a host of theorists from different polities who have experienced dilemmas of strategic choice in diverse circumstances.

Readers can be confident that what is revealed in table 3.1 is true for today and excludes claims that evidently reflect only their specific context. Overall, although I consider this table to be a reliable guide to understanding of strategy today, this draft of a general theory needs to be understood as most probably valid for a particular period in time. The theory has been selected with longevity in mind, but strategic – or even anti-strategic – history might surprise us. Because it is a 'living' theory, the understanding of strategy outlined here is subject to this author's evolving idea about the requirements of a general theory. To that end, table 3.1 formally incorporates a requirement for strategists to be as well informed about matters relevant to their national security duties as possible. However, I have determined that the requirement for Intelligence, stated here as Dictum 12, must only be pursued responsibly. A poorly disciplined search for danger may itself stimulate anxieties abroad that were better left unprovoked. While it is entirely proper for an Intelligence community to be alert to foreign peril, there is often need for some restraint in acknowledged speculation about dangers from abroad. For a collection of closely related ideas on a subject

**Table 3.1** The General Theory of Strategy in Twenty-three Dicta

**Nature and character of strategy**
1. Grand strategy is the direction and use made of any or all of the assets of a security community, including its military instrument, for the purposes of policy as decided by politics.
2. Military strategy is the direction and use made of force and the threat of force for the purposes of policy as decided by politics.
3. Strategy is the only bridge built and held to connect policy purposefully with the military and other instruments of power and influence.
4. Strategy serves politics instrumentally by generating net strategic effect.
5. Strategy is adversarial; it functions in both peace and war, and it always seeks a measure of control over enemies (and often over allies and neutrals, too).
6. Strategy usually requires deception, is frequently ironic, and occasionally is paradoxical.
7. Strategy is human.
8. The meaning and character of strategies are driven, though not dictated and wholly determined, by their contexts, all of which are constantly in play and can realistically be understood to constitute just one unified super-context.
9. Strategy has a permanent nature, while strategies (usually plans, formal or informal, expressing contingent operational intentions) have a variable character, driven but not mandated by their unique and changing contexts, whose needs are expressed in the decisions of individuals.

**Making strategy**
10. Strategy typically is made by a process of dialogue and negotiation.
11. Strategy is a value-charged zone of ideas and behaviour.
12. The making of strategy should always be informed by an understanding gleaned from overt and covert sources of Intelligence. This necessary activity must be ever alert to the perils of disinformation created by adversaries.
13. Historically specific strategies often are driven, and always are shaped, by culture and personality, while strategy in general theory is not.

**Table 3.1**  continued

---

**Executing strategy**

14. The strategy bridge must be held by competent strategists.
15. Strategy is more difficult to devise and execute than are policy, operations and tactics: the making and conduct of strategy inevitably create friction of all kinds.
16. The structure of the strategy function is best explained as comprising political ends, chosen ways and enabling means (especially, but not exclusively, military), and the whole endeavour is informed, shaped, and may even be driven, by the reigning assumptions, both those that are recognized and those that are not.
17. Strategy can be expressed in strategies that are: direct or indirect; sequential or cumulative; attritional or manoeuvrist–annihilating; persisting or raiding (more or less expeditionary); or a complex combination of these alternatives.
18. All strategies are shaped by their particular geographical contexts, but strategy itself is not.
19. Strategy is an unchanging, indeed unchangeable, human activity in thought and behaviour, set in a variably dynamic technological context.
20. Unlike strategy, all strategies are temporal.
21. Strategy is logistical.
22. Strategic theory is the most fundamental source of military doctrine, while doctrine is a notable enabler of, and guide for, strategies.

**Consequences of strategy**

23. All military behaviour is tactical in execution, but must have operational and strategic effect, intended and otherwise.

---

such as strategy's general theory, and given that there exists no truly authoritative theory, aspiring theorists can only deploy or deduce dicta that they find persuasive, leaving modern and subsequent theorists to decide whether or not they will endorse the latest version of the theory. For example, I am convinced that the general theory cannot be regarded as complete without formal recognition of the contribution that should be made by Intelligence. However, that recommendation has to be offered with an important explicit caveat regarding reliability.

This theory of strategy might warrant criticism for offering only a pre-theory which side-steps the need to reveal specific preferences. Although this critique would be a fair comment, it is important to comprehend strategy within the framework of a general theory that excludes any hint of authorial strategic preference. The beginning of wisdom on the seemingly enduring subject of strategy is to be found only by appreciating what is on offer and, by implication, the scale of potential disaster that can flow from poor choice. The overriding purpose behind this general theory (or pre-theory) has to be education, not policy advice for allegedly necessary practice. The general theory educates but should not attempt to advise on specific decisions. However, the chances of strategic practice being successful are increased when responsible officials understand the realm of strategic choice in the terms presented here. If the general theory of strategy is not to mislead, it must be preserved intact as a framework that helps organize the real-world and real-time choice, but not as a vital shortcut into strategists' here-and-now. Of course, even politicians, officials and soldiers who appear well educated about strategy's general theory can still misuse this knowledge as the ill-found basis for unsound choices.

Historian Williamson Murray has explained why the greatest war in Ancient Greece has relevance for us today, and thus why Thucydides' history of that conflict between Athens and Sparta should be regarded as still living evidence of eternal features of the human political and moral condition. Murray argues that:

> Thucydides did indeed write a work of history 'done to last forever'. It is deeply imbued with a theoretical understanding of war, its conduct, and the terrible consequences that it produces. The sad record of 2,400-plus-a-few years since its completion is an endless repetition of the same pattern. Yet while *The History of the Peloponnesian War*

is of great importance in the twenty-first century, the
modern age is perhaps even less prepared than its original
audience for its deep and abiding insights.[6]

This heartfelt judgement offered by a contemporary
professional historian is quoted in order to highlight the
strength of the argument for our regarding all of history
as being subject to the logical authority of the general
theory of strategy. Although every period has seen each
general perform according to his unique context and circumstances, they have all had to accept the discipline that
lurks none too furtively in the general theory of strategy.
From Pericles to Petraeus, the subject is the same. Readers
are warned that this claim is not universally accepted as
true by all our contemporary strategic thinkers.


## Theory and Practice

The great Prussian theorist of war, Carl von Clausewitz,
explained clearly that the primary function of theory – at
least of the rare kind of general theory that was his forte
– was education and not training. His master work, *On
War*, lays bare the nature of war and warfare, but not in
order to prescribe preferred methods or the most suitable
solutions for the policy, and hence the strategic, dilemmas
of the day. Obviously, a book written with many interrup-
tions in the late 1810s and through the 1820s could have
little, if anything, of significance to say directly about the
challenges to strategists in the twenty-first century. As with
Thucydides' writing of the Greek experience in the late
fifth century BC, Clausewitz was addressing problems that
endure – problems, so to speak, 'with legs'! Understandably, what the Prussian offered has not been what desper-
ate politicians and generals believe they lack, which is
practical solutions to the immediate challenges of their
day. General strategic theory is invaluable for what it alone
can provide, but it fades into the background when

soldiers must confront pragmatic difficulties. To explain more clearly, Clausewitz is quite explicit in warning soldiers that:

> Theory cannot equip the mind with formulas for solving problems, nor can it mark the narrow path on which the sole solution is supposed to lie by planting a hedge of principles on either side. But it can give the mind insight into the great mass of phenomena and of their relationships, then leave it free to rise into the higher realms of action. There the mind can use its innate talents to capacity, combining them all so as to seize on what is *right* and *true* as though this were a simple idea formed by their concentrated pressure – as though it were a response to the immediate challenge rather than a product of insight.[7]

In his most explicit explanation of the role of theory, Clausewitz makes abundantly clear that 'a theory need not be a positive doctrine, a sort of *manual* for action':[8]

> Theory will have fulfilled its main task when it is used to analyse the constituent elements of war, to distinguish precisely what at first sight seems fused, to explain in full the properties of the means employed and to show their probable effects, to define clearly the nature of the ends in view, and to illuminate all phases of warfare in a critical enquiry. Theory then becomes a guide to anyone who wants to learn about war from books, it will light his way, ease his progress, train his judgment, and help him avoid pitfalls.[9]

We are warned that even the theorist's principles and rules are intended to provide a thinking man with a frame of reference for the movements he has been trained to carry out, rather than to serve as a guide which, at the moment of action, lays down precisely the path he must take![10] It is plain to see that the most senior of authors on the nature of war and strategy does not intend to provide specific battlefield or campaign instruction. Clausewitz understood that the purpose of general theory is to educate the practising strategist so that he is fit to make the pragmatic decisions for which he is responsible. In practice, this means some translation of general precepts like those in the general theory (in table 3.1) into specific requirements particular to a geographical context – or probably several – and distinctively relevant to a unique strategic environment. In other words, the practising informed strategist must ask 'What does the general theory alert me to attend to, and why?' The theory warns the military professional of the likely nature of the problems he will have to face. Such recognition, though, offers no guarantee that workable solutions will be found. For example, in Afghanistan in the 2000s, although one may condemn apparent intellectual and political shortcomings on the NATO side, it is rather more persuasive to argue that no measure of official comprehension of the mixture of difficulties encountered would have served well enough to fuel substantial progress in Afghan security.[11] There are some political missions that cannot achieve success with any bearable burden of military effort, and prudence in policy and strategy is needed to prevent forlorn attempts to achieve the impossible.

While it should always be helpful to understand the problems of the day in terms of general theory, the fact must remain that such understanding, on its own, never provides crucial answers. Obviously, not all strategic challenges are conceptual. In 1916–17, Lord Kitchener's New Army simply lacked the tactical and technical skills to defeat the German Army. That happier condition was not attained until late in the summer of 1918.[12] Moving forward in time, the British Army lacked both the quality and the quantity necessary to be competitive in battle with the Wehrmacht of 1940–3, and, throughout the Second World War, it never managed to reach the heights of excellence achieved in the '100 days' campaign of Autumn 1918.[13] The British victory at El Alamein in 1942 was important, but it was won against an Afrika Korps hugely overwhelmed materially and in human assets.

Domestic political realities can result in what has to be recorded as strategic failure. No matter how sound the Western understanding of COIN (counterinsurgency) theory, or how much COIN practice improved, when the electorates of intervening states lose patience with, and interest in, particular political-strategic problems, the venture (or adventure) is effectively over.[14] The result will often be what looks like – and probably is – a variant of behaviour that we can classify unkindly but truthfully as 'scuttle and run'.

Both Thucydides and Clausewitz, with the emphasis they placed upon *tyche* – or chance – understood very well that the practice of strategy is apt to be hindered by unpredictable factors about which it can do nothing. The whole history of strategy illustrates the extensive range of elements that may hamper what looks as if it should have been a direct march towards intended goals. Winnable wars, sustainable peace, reliable allies – all have the potential to fail in historical practice, despite contemporary evidence of high confidence in theoretical understanding. Politicians and strategists would seem to be irresistibly seduced by the naïve promise of certainty about the future.

## National (and Cultural) Context

The drafting of general theory on strategy has been very much the exception and not the rule. Predictably enough, we strategists have tended to stick more or less closely to what can best, if unflatteringly, be seen as a tribalist tendency. When we look at strategic history, with its plethora of exciting, challenging and even desperately perilous 'moments', we discover only a modest canon of classic and more popular texts. Even the very few works that are generally acknowledged across cultural and other boundaries as having the status of classics, are in fact quite heavily loaded in favour of particular strategic assumptions that do little to stimulate debate on general theory. Hovering uneasily – waiting uncomfortably for introduction into the argument of this book – is the fact that, too often, strategic truth is most enthusiastically recognized, and realized in strategic practice, when it is produced in recognizable cultural garb.[15] My claim is not that strategic argument ought to take a form other than the one most prevalent, but rather that its production seems unable to transcend the boundary perceived and the pressures felt due to then-contemporary anxieties; moreover, those contemporary anxieties are almost all specific to time, place and geography. The subject here, after all, is not a matter for disinterested investigation by people, and sometimes institutions, untroubled by worldly concerns. Strategy, including its theory for strategic practice, has, by definition, always related to the most important issues of the day, or of the predicted near-future. Therefore, it is scarcely surprising that strategic theorists from all areas of expertise and all cultures, have written most eloquently about the security anxieties that beset their local society. They have written about strategic issues framed in a context to which their contemporaries could easily relate. Given that writings over literally millennia have been drafted primarily not in the scientific spirit of an Omniscient Observer seeking truth, but rather as intended contributions to what is understood at the time to be the public good, works on strategic theory have tended to be heavily 'presentist', about the author's and reader's 'now'. Theorists have sought to influence distinctly contemporary debate and action regarding the security problems of their day.

I recommend that readers try to take quite a long-term view of strategic history, including that of their own nation or tribe. If they do – even though it can be difficult – amidst the sound and fury of current local debate on policy matters, they should be able to discern the integrity claimed here for a general theory of strategy. There are many competing accounts of the advantages and alleged disadvantages of rival ideas for strategy and actual military posture, and it can be difficult to choose among them. Usually it helps to try to see the structure of the general theory of strategy that lies beneath – often inadvertently concealed by – the strategies devised to cope with specific short-term anxieties. A short-termist, even presentist, concern can undermine the prudence in judgement that general theory should encourage. Of course, general theory must never be over-specific – if it is, it will defeat its object and become a contradiction in terms – but its existence should never be neglected as a vital tool for education.

Strategic theory needs to be free of local and strictly contemporary geographical and cultural content if it is to be adaptable for the education of all. However, just as it can always be said to require the 'wearing of a dollar sign', so it always reflects the more or less obvious principal geographical – and hence geostrategic – assumptions of its authors.[16] Since strategic theory – even in its rare general form – is not the product of divine revelation, since all would-be strategic theorists lived in societies with particular strategic geographies, and since those geostrategic historical co-ordinates invariably come with distinctive, potentially dangerous strategic issues, we are blessed with a theoretical literature that is typically a light-year distant from general truth. Because this is a book about strategy and not a detailed examination of the national (*inter alia*) roots of state behaviour, by and large I will not comment on the motives behind statecraft. However, it is necessary to recognize here that, although scholars remain divided on most matters of international security, they are more or less united in agreeing with the commonsense proposition that enduring national strategic geography – location – encourages persisting tendencies in strategic thought and behaviour.[17] Behind these words lie more than thirty years of largely academic debate on the subject of strategic culture – or, put another way, culture and strategy.[18] Since 1977, at least, scholars in many countries have debated the proposition that different political cultures, typically demarcated by national borders, manifest different long-term preferences in strategic thought and behaviour. The reasons for these differences have been debated, but the claim persists that societies' strategic historical experiences leave what amounts to a cultural marking, even signature, on their strategic DNA! The argument comes in weak or strong forms and it has been directly challenged on the grounds that it lacks evidence. Above all, perhaps, this lack of evidence can be put down to the plausibility of alternative explanations of the course of strategic history. Nonetheless, the idea that there is an enduring, largely national, strategic cultural DNA has survived scholarly assault – even if only just. I have shifted my view towards recognizing the strong likelihood that some national memories, including legends and even myths, should be appreciated as notably cultural and therefore substantially enduring. However, this doesn't mean that strategic cultural influence is able to shape the course of national strategic choice. Despite this, efforts by some scholars to sink the concept and associated theory of strategic culture beyond recovery have plainly failed.

Despite some frustration concerning the frequent ambiguity of evidence on motivation for political and strategic choice, many, if not most, scholarly strategists recognize that there are often prevailing national patterns in strategic choice. Strategy has a secure future not only for systemic reasons that will not change – assuming appropriate caution is exercised in the area of nuclear strategy – but also due to many continuities in strategies that can be termed cultural. We are able with high confidence not only to predict a healthy future for strategy, but also to anticipate much about strategic choice. Always provided we allow for the possibility of accidents, chance events that have dire consequences, and occasionally eccentric official thought and behaviour by responsible people in key decision-making positions, there is good reason to believe that the future of strategy is most likely to be realized in the twenty-first century along lines, and in pursuit of goals, already well traced historically. Notwithstanding the undoubted relevance and occasional reality of the still popular, if rather vague, concept of globalization, a dominant political fact for today is the continuing authority of the nation state as, in theory and in practice, the commanding player on the world chess board. Moreover, not only is globalization a significantly limited practical reality in contemporary international relations, also it looks as if it will remain subordinate to the political authority of states for many decades to come. This unavoidable conclusion has important implications for the argument here.

The limitations on the globalization of security that we can safely assume have to mean that the historically known, or knowable, world is going to continue into the future, pretty much as it is now. For example, I am arguing not only that Russia will continue with strategic thought and behaviour, but also that there are powerfully persuasive reasons why those ideas and occasional actions are likely to be new, or apparently new, variants on choices of a kind Russia has been making for a long time. The Cold War is now a generation in the past and even the post-Cold War period seems exhausted, but in 2014 the Russia led by its new 'tsar' – to all intents and purposes, Vladimir Putin – is energetically pursuing distinctively traditional Russian policy goals in no less distinctively a brutish Russian manner. That said, it should not be surprising to find that Russia today is pushing back vigorously against the reduction of its power base that led to its effective demotion from superpower status in 1991.[19]

Within the highly abstract framework provided by the general theory of strategy, practising strategists are obliged to do their duty in designing, and perhaps putting into action, strategies specific to their historical situations. These serving strategists must devise and direct strategies that meet the specific anxieties and desires of their individual societies. Although the history of strategy is honoured by a few distinguished classic contributions from diverse political and cultural sources, it is necessary to recognize that these strategists most typically wrote, and certainly acted, for a mainly domestic audience. Anyone can read Carl von Clausewitz or Mao Tse-tung, but those strategists wrote primarily for a respectively Prussian or Chinese attentive public, and they theorized from the perspective of an insider in a political community assumed to share many of their values. Both strategic writings and strategic behaviour through the centuries and across continents have usually carried a clear political and cultural signature. We must allow for occasional eccentricity in strategic theoretical speculation, and for quite unanticipated events that appear to trigger culturally inconsistent responses. But there is unmistakeable evidence of a clustering of issue-areas in time and place that provide the principal foci for strategic speculation and debate.

It has often been claimed that, in modern times, nations, not armies, go to war. The leading strategic theorists of a generation in any country tend not to devote themselves unduly to the scholarly and often apparently irrelevant – to contemporary issues of policy and strategy – realm of strategy's general theory, because they must inhabit an actual national space in history, geography, technology and presumed menace, that always seems to need their expert services. Career rewards follow provision of useful advice now on the problems that officials, and possibly the public also, decide need expert strategic treatment. Such is the continuity in strategic history that, understandably, the particular geography and culture most relevant to perceived strategic anxiety and opportunity can stretch far back in time. This is not surprising given the several major and many minor revolutions in pertinent technologies wrought over the past two centuries. Geography is the most important factor that influences societies' political, and hence strategic, attitudes and choices worldwide. Technologies wax and wane in their perceived ability to encourage fear or ambition, but there is a bedrock of apparent eternity about a polity's established location and essential dimensions on the map. It is important to recognize the persisting reality of strategic thought, both as the historically particular response of theorists who find themselves locked into a specific space and time and are obliged to address more or less 'presentist' anxieties, and as the theoretical work of those very few able to transcend their contemporary contexts and educate prospectively for all time. Thucydides, for a leading example, sought explicitly to achieve the latter. However, even if an ambitious theorist is hoping for a place among the ten greatest strategic theorists of all time (in whose estimation?), his elevated wisdom will still be coloured by many assumptions that he may well not be aware he had made, but which place immovable political, cultural and historical markers on his work. Of course, the finest writers are able to raise their game above the grubby squabbles of their 'today', but, nonetheless, there is always a kind of indelible DNA suffusing strategic theory.

There really are no objective and politically disinterested expert strategic theorists: the closest to such were Thucydides and Clausewitz, who are still accessible to us. Because strategic theorists always allow – even if they do not encourage – political application or embrace, and because the wheels of governance everywhere always demand practical advice on the issues of today, even a preference for offering general wisdom on strategy is hard to sustain. Not only are would-be strategic theorists in effect bribed by the temptation of some access to power, but also, as encultured persons, they are bound to regard themselves as team players in the issues of contemporary strife against other encultured teams of rivals. Even when scholars perceive systemic peril – security dilemmas, for example[20] – in arrangements for national security, they will be unable to divest themselves completely of the emotional and material commitments they cannot easily, or prudently, avoid making. The scholarly strategist, even when bent upon a quest for truth, will have a family, a home, and some cultural acquisitions that are too deep to set aside readily as elements in his relevant world. Besides general theory about strategy, though, there are specific strategies chosen to meet the anxieties of the day, place and circumstance – these often come with some unavoidable cultural markers. Consideration of culture cannot be regarded as a reliable predictor of strategic thought and prospective practice, but it invariably plays a role in strategic decision-making, and that can be significant indeed. One classic historical example must be the relative significance of the territorial integrity of neutral Belgium in 1914. Britain did not join the Great War because Germany invaded Belgium; anxieties about the future balance of power were much more weighty than were concerns for international law.[21] However, Germany's brutal misbehaviour towards Belgium in August 1914 triggered widespread public anger in Britain and that encouraged British political leaders to justify their decision to fight in terms they could be completely confident would meet with public political and – above all – moral approval. This was a momentous occasion when a 400-year tradition of opposition to the ownership of the Low Countries by a continentally dominant Great Power was enhanced by an outburst of genuine moral outrage. Most polities have cultures that identify specific geographical locations as having allegedly deep meaning for their national security. For example, in addition to its obvious practical relevance for contemporary governance, greater Moscow has long been understood as having special cultural significance for most Russians: recognition of this perception was apparently the principal guide to British nuclear targeting strategy during the Cold War.[22] Reasoning with similar cultural content is relevant to most conflicts in history.

## The Value of Strategic Theory

Former Special Forces ('Green beret') soldier and later professor Harold D. Winton has provided the most useful basic structural guide to the value of theory. He advises, simply, that theory should *define* its subject, *categorize* the subject's more important parts and *explain* how the subject works.[23] In addition, theory should *connect* the subject with other relevant subjects, and possibly *anticipate* future behaviour. Winton is writing about military theory, but his approach is also valuable for strategy. Readers must judge for themselves just how useful the Winton norms for theory can be; personally, after many decades of teaching and writing I have yet to stumble across a more helpful summary guide.

It may be objected that an aversion to theory is widespread among both professional soldiers and politicians; these typically are pragmatic people far more interested in hearing what to do now, than in being told *how* they might improve performance by understanding the workings of their problems. In his outstanding biography of Field Marshal Sir Douglas Haig, Gary Sheffield explains how and why the culture of the military profession is seldom friendly to the employment of theory – at least it certainly was not in Britain before the First World War. Sheffield argues as follows: 'British military culture, rooted in attitudes in wider society, laid much emphasis on individualism and "character", which resulted in a cult of pragmatism, flexibility and an empirical approach relying on experience, not theory. The consequence was a "muddle through mentality" resistant to prescriptive doctrine. Haig was not immune to that influence.'[24]

This quotation reminds us that the story here is very much a human one and not a mechanical or even philosophical one. The working logic of strategy has to be made manifest in thought and actions only through human effort. When considered as a force of nature, it loses most of the potential reality needed in a subject involving situationally appropriate action. The basic structure of the general theory of strategy cannot operate as a 'hidden hand' of strategic history. It should serve to remind would-be practising strategists to be prudent – to focus on consequences – in their strategic decisions, but they can simply ignore strategy's logic. The strategic history of most polities, ancient, medieval and modern, is heavily laden with seriously mismatched quantities and qualities among ends, ways and means. Also, even when the theory of strategy is understood, and perhaps when there are serious efforts to put on a coherent strategic performance, there cannot be any worthwhile guarantee of success. Strategy is difficult to perform successfully, not least because enemies also need and often attempt to shine strategically. Theory is important as a source of advice for necessary discipline, but it is nothing like an independent source of strength; it has to be applied by naturally flawed and typically stressed executives.

# − 4 −

# Strategic History: Continuity and Change

There has always been a strategic quality to our human history. Its intensity has varied greatly, but unfortunately it has always been present. The fundamental reason for this is that our common need for security obliges us to behave politically, and that in its turn, in a structurally anarchic world, demands strategic performance on our part. There is no practical alternative. My intention in this chapter is to explain the genuinely mixed message that our history records both great continuities and cumulatively significant change. However, it is clear enough to me that the basic logic of strategy has been the same at all times and in all places, from the days of togas and chariots to those of modern business suits and high-precision weapons. This is not merely an assumption on my part, because the evidence for strategic behaviour in history is both continuous and overwhelming. As we will see, it is possible − indeed necessary − to view history from a strategic perspective. This is not to claim that strategy either has been or should be the dominant element in historical understanding, but it is to argue that history without strategy is bound to be seriously deficient. Because some innovation has been common to all periods of our history, it is necessary to treat continuity and change as being generally complementary features of a history that always has some strategic content.

## An Important Concept

As far as I know, few professional historians have chosen to borrow and exploit the concept of strategic history. This relative neglect has led to our understanding of the strategic dimension to the past being needlessly restricted.[1] I do not agree with the view that strategy, regarded as a function essential to human life, is a distinctly modern invention. If what is understood widely today as strategy and strategic reasoning is not seriously in scholarly dispute, then it is only sensible, certainly it should be practicable, to consider how – or indeed whether – its scope has altered over time. I am convinced that all of our human past, and its sometimes controversial interpretation as history, has had a strategic dimension.[2] This dimension has, of course, been more or less important as historical circumstances altered, but it was never completely out of the picture. The reason should be obvious. Whether military menace was actual or anticipated as probable for the future, the nature of the strategic dimension to human affairs meant that it could never be dismissed as wholly irrelevant. We do not need to accept a narrowly – let alone a quasi-professional – military view of the full meaning of 'strategic', in order to grasp that recognition of this concept has always been a vital necessity for secure human life.

We need to understand the vital concept of security as fully as we can. Strategy in its current meaning, along with the whole subject known today as Strategic Studies, stems from the feelings of insecurity that both individuals and groups have always harboured, needlessly or not. In practice, the unravelling of strategic history can be hindered by the fact that few scholars appear ready to tackle the complex idea of continuity with change. For me, recognition of the following 'working parts' is essential.

1. The past has always had a strategic dimension.
2. The strategic dimension to history has been, still is and probably always will be a permanent feature of human existence.
3. Because we see human existence as always needing a security that will let us arrange our social and political lives how we want, we are obliged – for lack of anything better – always to watch for potential dangers of a strategic kind. By this we mean dangers that could lead to forms of coercion by force: these perils – actual or potential – can have an explicitly military character.
4. The logic behind, indeed driving, this itemization of the reasons for concern, does not just apply to particular times, places or circumstances; rather, I am presenting an understanding that is relevant to all human social life. Such life is necessarily both political and, to a greater or lesser extent, strategic.

So great are the changes from the past that it is no easy matter to convince those who are sceptical that there is vital continuity despite change, as well as change in continuity. The evidence of change can be so obvious that it encourages scholars and officials to be unwisely dismissive of what they may well consign to the garbage bin as having, because of its age, no relevance for understanding of the present and future. It makes sense to be wary of the dangers of true antiquarianism. Past beliefs, habits and practices may be valued for no better reason than their age and apparent distinguished provenance. The late fifteenth-century Italy of Niccolò Machiavelli was as impressed by classical Roman examples of military excellence – both those well evidenced and others that were not – as were

Benito Mussolini and his *fascisti* five centuries later.[3] Some ancient military practices were not merely sound, but actually vital enablers for the contemporary need for strict discipline and careful drill in the generation of gunpowder-fuelled firepower. The practical challenge that we have to recognize is the need to find and adapt old ideas and practices, while consigning inappropriate ones from the past to permanent occupancy only of the library and museum. Irritated rejection of the old, simply because it is old, can be as foolish as overexcitement about the new, because it is new.

There is no mystery here, because the complex ideas of continuity and change that have graced these pages already contain both the kernel of the issue and the most appropriate solution. One needs to link actual and proposed change closely with understanding of what needs to continue. Probably the best way to approach this difficult task is by distinguishing clearly between the enduring nature of a subject and its ever-shifting character. In this book, I demarcate clearly between the general theory of strategy and specific strategies, meaning the choices appropriate to particular circumstances and kinds of military assets. Obviously, there is a certain amount of fusion of the general and the particular. However, one should be able to give a stripped-down strategy presentation to an audience from any military culture of any time or place, and hope it will make sense. Naturally, this may overstate the case somewhat, and even if the presentation is delivered fluently in the appropriate language, it would still probably sound strange and hard to understand. Nonetheless, the idea is plain enough. A general theory of strategy should cover the relevant subjects in ways that should be deemed valid by any audience.

The beginning of wisdom on strategy should be acceptance of the key concept of strategic history. This overarching concept serves crucially to justify borrowing from, and much commentary on, different times and places. Of course the idea of strategic history entails some highly controversial issues. Probably the most obvious is that of anachronism. To clarify: how can one aspire to explain Julius Caesar's strategic thought and behaviour if in practice we are only able to apply 21st-century reasoning? How much can we trust our ability to interpret his thought and behaviour? We have a reasonable amount of evidence of events upon which to draw, but how reliable are the conclusions we draw from this?[4] Readers may have guessed where this is taking us. What I am suggesting is that the evidence of strategically significant deeds and misdeeds can be assumed well enough today. Provided we only want to gain an historical understanding of strategy that is 'good enough' to fit with the particular context of the times in question, we should be reasonably content with the strategic historical understanding that we can achieve today. We need to understand that strategic and military cultures have altered significantly over time and across geography. But the general theory of strategy can accommodate unusual phenomena quite well. Indeed, if exceptional thought and behaviour appear to begin to menace the plausibility of strategy's general theory, it is more likely to be a consequence of indiscipline in theorizing. Advocates of novelty in tactics and operational artistry frequently strive to crawl onto the pages of general strategy, and their devotees are likely to believe that their hope for a strategic revolution is sufficient to make it a reality.

## What Changes, and What Does Not?

Because the broad subject of strategy is always likely to alter in detail, it can be challenging to keep track of what does not change, and why that is so. The general theory provides background understanding to the strategists and commanding generals who need to know what is, and what is not, best current tactical practice. Because every war is unique, it is imprudent to assume that 'one size fits all' in tactical military competence. One size typically does not fit many cases of conflict.[5] However, emphasis on being adaptable and flexible should help prepare the way for the better tailoring of force to particular cases of coercive need.[6] Arguably, the wisest words in Clausewitz' *On War*, are the following:

> *First*, it is clear that war should never be thought of as something *autonomous* but always as an instrument of policy; otherwise the entire history of war would contradict us. Only this approach will enable us to penetrate the problem intelligently. *Second*, this way of looking at it will show us how wars must vary with the nature of their motives and of the situations which give rise to them.
>
> The first, the supreme, the most far-reaching act of judgment that the statesman and commander have to make is to establish by that test the kind of war on which they are embarking; neither mistaking it for, nor trying to turn it into, something that is alien to its nature. This is the first of all strategic questions and the most comprehensive.[7]

However, as the Prussian well knew, although war can and indeed needs to be understood as a distinctive form of collective human behaviour, it is eminently capable of shifting its internal shape. While we do need to be clear about what we mean by war, we should also be alert to variation in categorical emphasis that could lead us astray politically and analytically.[8] Clausewitz identified what should be regarded as mandatory truths of the first order. But, what he did not cover with the necessary subtlety was the all-but organic, living and evolving quality of war.[9] It is essential to be clear about the subordination of organized force to political purpose, and its need to reflect the intensity of that purpose. But, the long record of warfare shows overwhelming evidence of the unpredictable consequences of unexpected military events. Despite what Clausewitz rightly says about the instrumentality of military happenings – that they can be seen as the product of a process of purposeful strategic interaction – it is not entirely wrong to think of war as a dynamic struggle, whose course and outcome can be neither pre-scripted nor anticipated with high confidence.

Although move and countermove can be the foci of military planners' best efforts, the fact remains that war has always been the supreme game of chance, as Clausewitz himself noted.[10] On the level of theory, Clausewitz unquestionably was correct, and what he wrote should be heeded with respect. However, that respect should not be permitted to dominate all of our understanding of war, regardless of the different emphases that can have profound consequences. We clearly need to recognize the variety of forms that war and warfare can take. To avoid public misunderstanding of what is going on in a war zone, there should be constant reminders of the political purpose behind the fight. But strategists on all sides also need to be willing to shift the emphases of the violence they license and execute, in order to respond to the circumstances of conflict in which they find themselves.

In practice, the doing of strategic history is more of a creative activity than a long-planned one. Popular commentators err frequently in their efforts to explain the course of strategically meaningful events when they fail to understand the degree to which war and warfare require the ability to exploit unanticipated success and also to survive unexpected military failure. War is a journey into the unknown. The most central of reasons for this condition is so obvious that it all but escapes notice. Specifically, as Clausewitz explains, 'War is nothing but a duel on a larger scale.'[11] This is an eternal truth about war, but it is one that policymakers and strategists are often tempted to ignore or even dismiss out-of-hand. While it is entirely appropriate for me to flag for readers the endless litany of difficulties that can hinder, if not frustrate totally, strategic performance, it has been common for belligerents to appear to behave as if their enemies could be regarded substantially as passive objects.[12] Once appreciation of the nature of strategy is harnessed to a convincing grasp of enemies' range of options, one risks being unable to make decisions. As if the basic condition of both sides having strategic free will were not troubling enough for orderly minds, we also need to throw in a layering of circumstance that neither side reasonably could have anticipated, let alone predicted. As the great man wrote, 'War is the realm of chance.' To which we should add 'and of surprise also'.

All of this serves to emphasize the frightening degree to which chance and unpredictable consequences are locked into the nature of strategy in international statecraft and, indeed, war. Of course, states and other combatants strive to anticipate reactions to their initiatives, but the risks and dangers can be hard, if not impossible, to comprehend in advance. It may be objected that, by and large, it does not much matter if strategists make mistakes in their predictions, because some rapid course correction is usually feasible. Unfortunately, this relaxed view of statecraft and strategy is not without hazard. The idea of prudence looms so large over strategic history because the record of happenings shows unmistakeably that errors in policy and strategy often have lethal consequences. Williamson Murray is persuasive when he argues that political and strategic error is apt to be impossible to correct – not that it is often attempted – given the all-too-human tendency of leaders to minimize the rather obviously dire consequences of their mistakes.[13] It is plain to see that German policy in both 1914 and 1939–41 was very much mistaken. Similarly – though fortunately on a more modest scale – there were grave errors in American policy and strategy concerning Vietnam in the mid and late 1960s, and also with respect to Iraq and Afghanistan in the 2000s. The basic architecture of the theory of strategy, employing the conceptual quartet of ends, ways, means and assumptions, might have triggered reassessments that should have ruled out the likelihood of gross error, but of course it could not and did not. The reason was that the German and American strategic errors to which I refer were not the product of a culture-neutral analytical machine; rather, they were political and strategic judgements made very much in the grip of false assumptions and unrealistic assessments of the ability of available military means to be employed in sufficiently effective ways to realize the ends of political ambition.

An important goal for this text is to persuade the reader that strategic history has always shown a highly dynamic ability to yield unexpected outcomes. Although the future has to be the product of preceding elements, it can reveal itself in ways that are astonishing even to most 'expert' commentator-futurists. There is a reason why our ability to foresee the future is prone to errors of all sizes.[14] The events of the twentieth century were not foreseen or, indeed, realistically foreseeable. The scope for individual and collective choice is too extensive to permit high confidence. This easily demonstrated condition does not discourage governments from seeking to peer into the future for their polity. This is particularly true for strategists. Despite the abundant evidence that points to the need for extreme caution in prediction, politicians and officials seem unable to resist the temptation to peer into crystal balls. Since crystal balls of scientifically proven (i.e. empirically tested) quality do not and cannot exist, officials have to make do with the best guesses of political bosses and the preferred, usually obedient, supposedly expert knowledge derived from sundry social scientific methods. The obvious absence of evidence from the future about the future renders the whole analytical industry of futurology close to useless, and possibly even dangerous.

This absence of data from the future is a possibly lethal weakness for the future of strategy. Once one recognizes the practical possibility, indeed the occasional occurrence, of unpredictable but deeply consequential 'black swan' events, the limitation inherent in the architecture of the theory of strategy almost begs to be noticed.[15] Specifically, the abstract linking of ends, ways and means is readily revealed as being of little disciplinary value if the key strategic concerns that it theorizes are prey to essentially political, and even personal, judgements. The German and

American alleged cases of erroneous strategic reasoning cited above were not necessarily traceable to error in strategic understanding. The point is that the course of strategic history produces dynamically opposed sets of assets and liabilities whose combatively combined strategic performance is hard to predict ahead of trial by fire in the field of action. Sometimes we forget that the future really cannot be foreseen. Moreover, course correction in policy and strategy is by no means always possible or necessarily prudent.

It is sensible to ask whether the adaptable abstract formula of ends, ways and means – fuelled by assumptions – is liable to cause more harm than good. After all, there is little use in an abstract strategy function which is threatened even by honest error. The German and American problems, respectively in the early 1940s and predominantly in the 1960s, could not have been much alleviated by improved strategic theory. The overarching problem for German strategic performance in the Second World War was the political ambition of the Führer. Because the Third Reich could generate armed forces with outstanding fighting qualities, the Führer's political desires were certain to drive the need for German strategic effectiveness both too far and too fast. But highly optimistic assumptions meant that the basic logic of ends, ways and means was not affronted – at least, for a while. Policy preference and decisions in most polities are forged by states' domestic processes a long way ahead of trial by battle.

We have to recognize the fact that the workings of the logic of strategy are entirely in the hands of those political decision makers. It follows that there is always going to be a severe limitation on the quality control that should be a result of the interdependent logic of strategy's basic theory. In reality, the abundant historical evidence from all periods and cultures attests to the strength of political will, not necessarily to the importance of comfortable fit among purpose, method, and military instrument. It follows that, while the abstract formula of ends, ways, means – and assumptions – has a persisting integrity through time and in diverse climes, it cannot possibly serve as a sufficiently effective matrix in guiding strategic thought and practice.

For example, in 1941–2 Adolf Hitler was convinced, on the basis largely of the USSR's evident weaknesses as a prospective belligerent, that it would only take a single campaign to cause the Soviet Union to collapse.[16] This was not an entirely foolish assumption on Hitler's part; indeed, most British and American expert observers thought the same. But it proved incorrect, and its official endorsement by Germany was fatal to Hitler's overall plan for conquest in the East. The scale of the errors in Germany's conflict assumptions in 1941 affected not only Hitler's policy and strategy designs, but also many related aspects of the German military effort. If the enemy is fundamentally despised on racial and cultural grounds, it is easy to accept deficiencies in one's own military capabilities as being essentially irrelevant: a few German military weaknesses should not preclude a successful outcome for the single campaign assumed to be sufficient to bring the entire rotten structure of Communism in Russia crashing down – if the Soviet enemy was as weak as German leaders believed.

For another example, moving forward in the course of history to America's adventurous decade characterized by interventions in Afghanistan and Iraq, it is all too easy to see why the logical structure of strategy was not enough to ensure Americans avoided making fatal strategic errors. An assumption of superpower strategic policy served to undermine American (and British) strategy that was good, if rather arrogant, in both Afghanistan and Iraq. In practice, the same lethal flaws recurred in the American approach(es) to both conflicts. America's policy ends for both countries were well intentioned, but unfortunately they were grossly disrespectful of key features of the local cultures. Because of the historical context of the Afghan and Iraqi ventures in American strategic history, the US strategic effort in both cases suffered unmistakeably from a potent variant of what afflicted Hitler's Third Reich in winter 1940–1 – 'victory disease'. The combination of American self-confidence in its golden strategic historical moment at the close of the 1990s, and a record of recent (if distinctly arguable) strategic success in the Balkans, misled Washington into unrecognized adoption of the assumption that America could accomplish almost any strategic task that it chose. Evidence of probable American error (e.g. too few boots on the local ground) did not prompt alarm, because it was assumed that America would be able to adapt and adjust as necessary to cope with unanticipated contingencies.

Both the German and the American cases just cited provide ample empirical evidence of the fatal damage that can be inflicted by false assumptions about the prospects for strategic success. It is important to flag definitively that this text is not hostile to the making of commanding assumptions. Because, by definition, the future has not happened and is always out of reach, the practical challenge to strategists worthy of the job title is how best to cope with the huge uncertainty that inevitably creates. I have sought to grapple with this difficulty for many years. As is so often the case, scholarship on this much vexed question yields both bad news and good. Since time travel continues to be beyond the reach of ever-hopeful physicists, we have to accept the limitations of even the most modern strands of science. The future is unknown and unknowable to us. However, we are indeed knowledgeable about our strategic future, thanks to our access to the – often contentious – claims made concerning our strategic past. In practice, the challenge we face is knowing what reasonably can, and what cannot, be sought as useful knowledge about the strategic future. Even if we cannot aspire to predict particular events, let alone their distinctly hypothetical second- or third-order consequences, what can we seek to know that plainly is knowable, and strategically just how useful ought that to be?[17]

# Two Hundred Years of Strategic History

It is frustrating to realize that while, on the one hand, we can enjoy firmly grounded – if sometimes controversial – understanding of the course of strategic history – the ancient, as well as the medieval and modern – in a way that remains meaningful, on the other hand we can draw no thoroughly reliable lessons from that understanding. The course of strategic history, though by no means lacking in generally positive developments, still has to be regarded as like a lethal machine that lacks necessary safety devices. Time and again, even if infrequently, the human race has behaved collectively in an apparently mass-suicidal manner. To date, throughout accessible and variably well enough recorded strategic history, collective political and strategic conflict has only had severe negative consequences for restricted locales on the planet. However, with the dawn of the age of airpower – now a global airpower – as well as of long-range missile power by the late 1950s, and, most notably of all, with the weaponization of atomic fission and fusion, the human potential to destroy, or at least poison, much of the global environment, natural and man-made, has come to stay.

It would be agreeable to be able to write sincerely about the huge ironic merit in nuclear armament.[18] After all, one might attempt to argue, the danger of nuclear war has to be judged so severe as to have altered the playbook of international politics and strategy. In other words, one can attempt to persuade oneself that nuclear facts have changed, beyond doubt, what had seemed to be the persisting actuality of a world politics locked inescapably by anarchy into war-readiness. Unfortunately, there is grim irony in the linked fact that it is the enduring severity of nuclear menace that enforces the necessary discipline upon human political (mis)behaviour. There are some scholars, largely in the more numerate of the social sciences, who believe that human strategic history has just about run its abominable course.[19] While a more ironic track allegedly is detectable in the relative rarity of episodes of major war over the past two centuries, there has been an understandably irresistible temptation to identify the dawn of the nuclear era as principal villain, but also with no little embarrassment as probably, if still potentially, the most significant force for peace in the contemporary world.

It is reasonably clear that the sudden appearance of nuclear weapons in action in August 1945 either changed – or threatened to – what was understood globally about the rules and risks of international politics. Prior to 1945 it was well understood that wars, even major wars, happened from time to time. Also, the war-prone condition was understood to be an enduring condition of menace necessary for international order and the preservation or restoration of the balance of power that was the most essential disciplinary element governing behaviour in the whole system of states. As a result of the military-technological leaps made from 1945 until the early 1960s, it came to be appreciated widely that world politics and therefore its strategy, either already had altered radically, or needed urgently to do so.[20] In other words, world politics and its strategy/ies had changed very noticeably and after only a very few years. One could speculate in the 1950s along the lines just suggested, but was it true? Had strategic history in effect cancelled itself out, by allowing the appearance of weapons that could not serve strategy prudently?[21]

As the initial frightening excitement faded somewhat in the 1960s – especially following the really terrifying experience of the acute Cuban Missile Crisis of October 1962 – many strategists came to appreciate that nuclear weapons appeared to be tameable as servants of strategy. Moreover, it began to be possible to take a longer-term view of the years since 1945, and to consider whether or not the strategic world truly had altered all that radically. I was educated in the 1950s and early 1960s, and was encouraged to regard all that had happened prior to August 1945 as being Ancient History, currently of merely antiquarian interest. But, by the mid to late 1960s, the nuclear era belatedly was semi-integrated into a coherent narrative of strategic history. Nuclear facts were not – indeed, could not be – denied or wilfully abolished by expedient universal fiat, but they could be fitted into what had to remain a noticeably still nuclear narrative for the global avoidance of nuclear war. This interpretation of nuclear actualities and beliefs continues in the next chapter, when I explain how the nuclear peril was arguably, and remains, tamed by strategy – though perhaps 'trained' would be a more suitable word.

It is probably useful to pose a fundamental question regarding our knowledge of strategic history. Must collective political experience always be matched by some strategic narrative? Put another way, is there anything to be learnt, by way of analogy, from the course of the Great Power war – in its principal years, 431–404 BC – that absorbed such an appalling measure of Athenian and Spartan wealth?[22] Leaving aside, for the moment, arguments among classical scholars today about bias and therefore reliability in Thucydides' *History of the Peloponnesian War*, did the Greek author describe and explain a political and strategic context for statecraft that has meaning for our today and tomorrow? If we consider strategic history before 1945 as being at least potentially relevant to us today, what has changed and what has not? More to the point, perhaps, are there severe practical limits to what can change, no matter how different the Ancient Greek world appears to us in material and cultural detail? These are troubling questions that cannot lightly be put aside *pro tem*, let alone dismissed as irrelevant. Has the weaponization of nuclear physics in effect rendered all that occurred prior to July–August 1945 irrelevant to the future course of history? Obviously, a positive answer to that question has to dismiss as a dangerous irrelevance any effort by us to reach back before 1945 for strategic historical education.

## Did Strategic History Have a Start Date?
## Could It End?

The individual strategist may well find inspiration in a vision of a better way of life, perhaps in the hope of increasing the security of his or her home-team polity. However, careful study of the lengthy narrative of the human past reveals plainly that there has never been an era anything like a Golden Age. Moreover, there are no grounds for assuming that a long-term condition of satisfactory security is feasible. If it isn't, this means that all of our collective and individual efforts on behalf of security, are just episodes in an endless human political story. It may come as a surprise to many readers to be told that, although the narrative of strategy in the past has had many outcomes, none of them have been permanent. I must add speedily that given the normal human lifespan, official decisions here or there, and even the roll of the dice of chance, can make an enormous difference to health, happiness and even mere longevity. Imagine you had some radically alternative potential birth date and national origin during the arbitrary period of 1890 to 1920, and consider what your life experiences might well have been. It is true that the first half of the twentieth century was unusual in being marred by large-scale conflict, but it is also true that perilous times have troubled us repeatedly.

It is a shame we have ample evidence to show that the core of difficulties over security in strategic history are not due merely to the making of poor social decisions by human beings, who inevitably have flawed judgement. Strategic history attests to the episodic return of tragedy on a grand scale largely because it could not be avoided. One can behave honourably, have morally good intentions, and be suitably respectful of the fundamental architecture of the theory of strategy (ends, ways, means – and assumptions), yet still permit, and even enable, undoubtedly tragic consequences to one's chosen actions. The true challenges for national and international security lie in the nature of the problem-set with which we must deal. This recognition commands the paying of deep respect to the nature of the subject here, and abandonment of hopes for a political path to a lasting condition of global security. All that this argument demands is that statecraft and strategy need to be ruled, or at least restrained, by the principle of prudence.

I am advancing the conservative proposition that the nature of the human enterprise is necessarily political, and therefore strategic. The nature – as opposed to the character – of our human political and strategic venture had no readily identifiable beginning, and has, we hope, no foreseeable overriding end.[23] The vision industry of futurologists of diverse stripes of hope will not approve of this argument. After all, it appears to be merely an inconclusive future narrative – if we are successful in crisis management. The two concluding chapters of this book attempt to explain the size of the challenge of providing enhanced human security. Again and again, however, the text insists that readers accept as highly probable that there is no 'promised land' in the future, only a troubled time with dangerous episodes that require appropriate mastery of the theory and practice of strategy if the human race is to survive.

# − 5 −

# Strategy, Strategies, and Geography

I suspect that a significant reason for the evident difficulty many people have in understanding strategy lies in the indiscriminate way in which the term is bandied about. The purpose of this chapter is to disentangle the concept from much of the confusion that can obscure it, largely with reference to the geographical factor. In this book, I explain two meanings of strategy. On the one hand, there is strategy the function, presented in the twenty-three dicta of my general theory; while, on the other hand, there is strategy meaning a specific plan to achieve a particular result in unique circumstances. Strategists typically need to be familiar with the general theory of the function of strategy, in order to be able to design and direct a specific strategy in the material and psychological realm of contemporary military action.

For example, when I argue that Air Chief Marshal Dowding had a strategy in the summer of 1940, I mean that: (1) he devised a plan for the air defence of Great Britain that had clear political purpose (to deny the Luftwaffe the kind of victory that might plausibly compel Britain to surrender); (2) he chose a way to fight in the air that seemed adequate to deny victory to the Luftwaffe; (3) since 1936 he had prepared the combat instrument that was RAF Fighter Command for warfare of the kind that proved necessary in 1940; and (4) he was fortunate in the key assumptions he made about the probable course and consequences of a German air assault. In short, Dowding proved to be a true strategist, planning and directing action in the first occurrence in all strategic history of a stand-alone (there was no ongoing conflict on land at the time) air campaign.[1]

Strategies in the plural for real-world action, as contrasted with strategy as general theory, will have all the crucially important details added (or missing through neglect!) by people in the particular circumstances that have occasioned the need for appropriate strategy. The general theory cannot be stretched to answer 'How?' and 'With what?' questions specific to unique historical situations. How do we assault Hitler's European continental fortress – with what, precisely, should we attempt to do it? In similar fashion, the Third Reich had to determine how best it could defend its conquests, and with what military assets it should strive to do so?

The distinction between the general and the historically very specific is best explained on the basis of understanding the complementary, albeit hierarchical, needs involved. There is obvious need for both general theory and application of what it advises in an appropriate form to meet contemporary challenges. In 1944, General Eisenhower needed to have a general awareness of the logical interdependent structural elements in strategy's general theory (ends, ways, means and assumptions). That strategic education prepared and enabled him to command the invasion of continental Europe. A single general theory serves for the basic education of strategists around the world in conflict of all kinds.

## The General and the Particular

The strategic history of the human race exists in two complementary strands. On the one hand, it shows the persistent importance of the strategy function for political affairs, while on the other, it contains many historical examples of the particular elements of the strategy function in action. Although Clausewitz was persuasive in praising theory for its ability to help us in 'sorting out the material and plowing through it', what he failed to mention is the historical reality that people make the wrong choices.[2] However, he did indicate that the conduct of war cannot be reduced to an 'algebraic formula for use on the battlefield'.[3] Strategy in application always, without historical exception, requires translation from an abstract idea into a plan for action specific to time, place and circumstance. Like an athlete, a polity strives to choose and execute strategy that fits evident need. Because strategy is extraordinarily difficult to do well, it is often prudent to be willing to settle for a good enough standard of performance. Because strategic history is ongoing, it is easy to downplay its scale and the diversity of its practical challenges. It is important to master the theory of strategy, but only if it makes us better able to practise the art of strategy creatively in the unique context(s) of the day.[4] The most important features in the strategy designs of rival polities do not lend themselves to scientific analysis. Political actors obliged to perform strategically cannot helpfully simplify the most important elements discussed in any particular conflict. Even when there are features common to many different historical cases – perhaps crises, responses to attempts at coercion, or alliance reliability – it is always going to be sensible to leave some room for doubt. This doubt is due to the uncomfortable realization that while, on the one hand, strategic history always contains a recurring array of possibly dominant factors, on the other, every context is alarmingly unique.

I argue later in this chapter that it is impossible to prove scientifically whether a strategy will perform effectively. For a particularly troubling example, one cannot help but have doubts about the practice of strategy with nuclear weapons. In the First World War, some of the grosser errors committed each year could be addressed and to an extent put right through corrective strategic behaviour in the following year's effort (each year from 1914 to 1918). Such valuable, if expensively acquired, education in strategy is not likely to be matched in the course of nuclear warfare. Indeed, one of the more obvious characteristics of such warfare is its uselessness as learning experience. This is an important historically unique feature of the nuclear context. It would be most unlikely that learning time would be available, or could be earned by carefully applying pressure.

Only in the more narrowly focused of military history books and the more dedicated of would-be social scientific texts does strategy appear in the all-but-bloodless and emotion-lite guise of a calculable exercise. While the practice of strategy should find some inspiration in general theory, there is always need for the abstraction in apparently wise generality to be translated into a plan for threat and action today and tomorrow. The purpose of planning is to organize and assign duties strategically for intended effect. Usually it is advisable to approach strategic planning for national security as an exercise in what is known as grand strategy.[5] This ambitious concept aspires to provide guidance and control over all the assets of a polity for the purpose of achieving a collective effort, in pursuit of a large-scale strategic effect, in order to meet the overall challenge of the day. However, in practice, each polity will always have uneven strengths and relative weaknesses vis-à-vis the perils that it faces. Indeed, because each polity has a unique strategic history – one expressive of distinctive experience and physical geographical context – it is scarcely surprising to find also sharply different defence postures composed of military capabilities of variable competence.

## Geography, History, Politics

Why do polities select the national security strategy/ies that they do?[6] Firm answers may be hard to provide in the historical context of fairly common access to reasonably well understood technologies, and when budgetary pressures or strategic circumstances do not appear to be the deciding factors.

It is fair to say there are always many, often competing, pressures that demand political attention when polities must decide upon the shape and quality of their national security policies, especially regarding defence. Geography has always enjoyed pole position – and still does – as the principal influence on choices about national security. This enduring fact, which is too obvious to be disputed, still applies today, despite the cumulative and even revolutionary changes that have characterized the past two centuries. If we look first at what the influence of national geographical awareness means in broad terms, its scale and importance should soon become clear. I will hazard two bold claims:

1. Geography – both objective and subjective – explains more about a polity's national security issues than does any other factor – which is not quite to claim that it is determinative.
2. Geography typically provides the necessary explanation for why particular defence choices are made.

The history – not only strategic – of a polity lends itself to explanation that contains strong geographical content. Without attributing everything to geography, we should still recognize that geographical location must have profound implications for national security, and certainly for anxieties about it. In his *Arthashastra*, Kautilya offers advice about the advantages and dangers of a polity's neighbours.[7] As a general rule in international politics, it is common for neighbours to be enemies, while neighbours-but-one on the geopolitical chessboard of policy and strategy most typically are allies. Even when this is not quite the case at any specific moment, it is always going to be suspected of being likely to happen, and therefore it fuels ill feeling. After all, this is largely commonsense. Readers may recall that, all through the1980s, the People's Republic of China (PRC) chose to think and behave as if it was, in fact, an ally of the United States and of NATO. In that lengthy period, I discussed joint US and PRC strategic concerns with Chinese frontier commanders and there was a strong sense of substantially common strategic peril.[8] In the 1980s, the Soviet Union deployed approximately forty-two divisions on its border with China. For another major example in modern strategic history, Otto von Bismarck was acutely aware of the danger to the new German empire should it be obliged to plan for war on two radically divergent fronts, against France in the West and Russia in the East. Understanding of Germany's location helps to explain a great deal about German foreign policy and strategy from the 1870s until 1945.[9]

A country's geography must have a major influence upon its choices in strategy, and therefore, necessarily, in defence provision. Many polities buy military equipment specialized for operation in distinctive geographical contexts, but relatively few are seriously confused as to their primary geostrategic orientation. To risk some exaggeration in the interest of clarity, national security orientation can often be understood as mainly either continental or maritime. The aerial domain, more recently the nuclear-weapon realm and, more recently still, cyberspace, all offer greater or lesser challenges to the rather limited two geographical choices I have suggested. I suggest that the aerial domain has not achieved independent geostrategic dominance, at least not unless it is combined with the mission of nuclear delivery, which it owned exclusively in the United States from 1945 until 1960. As for cyberspace, we do not as yet have a confidently settled understanding of how the new technology can be used strategically. Cyber expertise is growing apace globally, and there is some experience of defence and some of offence, but the strategic meaning of the burgeoning technical and tactical competence remains very much a subject for exciting claims and counter-claims, most of them dubious.[10]

It is one thing to note a geographical preference revealed in a national security policy, but it is quite another to understand what the preference means strategically. For this purpose, it is necessary to venture into the ill-explored but appropriately elevated fields of grand strategy and geostrategy.

## Grand Strategy and Geostrategy

Scholars are not agreed on a dominant definition of grand strategy, while they are notably uncomfortable with the large and undefined idea of geostrategy. With that in mind, I will provide my own definitions and explanations. By 'grand strategy', I mean the direction and use made of any or all of the assets of a security community. This concept is less important than policy and the political process from which it must emerge. That said, grand strategy is nevertheless so important that few scholars or practitioners have been willing to try to clarify it. In my view, strategy is rendered grand not only because I judge it extraordinarily important, but also because its theoretical and practical scope needs to be understood to be all-embracing. In order to be grand, strategy needs to be capable of mobilizing any of a community's assets. As regards geostrategy, although strategy, per se, involves more than just particular physical geography, the strategies that are chosen have to be tolerant of geographical constraints, and preferably able to exploit favoured geographical contexts.

Readers will appreciate that it is necessary both to acknowledge the constraining potential of some geographical contexts – extreme distance, exceptionally rugged terrain, harsh climatic conditions – and to be careful not to be overly friendly to historical interpretations that allow physical geography to determine policy and strategy. Strategic history has shown that careless choice of policy occurs frequently: it can be spotted and categorized as a class of unusually hazardous decisions that have dire consequences. My intention here is only to point out that particular physical geographical contexts always play a part in strategic history, but it is important not to overstate that part. Yet scholarship in Strategic Studies and International Relations over the past half-century has been far too dismissive of its role. Of course, technology has challenged and can alter the meaning of physical geography (the Luftwaffe being only six minutes' warning time away from the British south coast in 1940 was an empirical detail that mattered critically).

Scarcely less important than the geographical factor are the ideas and even impulses which can be understood as broadly cultural.[11] In this text I wish to recognize the potency of ideas, as well as more material influences. Without getting too abstract, I still need to explain that strategy, grand or military, is more likely to be the product of the individual or even the collective imagination, and then of its attempted execution by the human will, than the result of careful analysis and debate. Because the future has not happened and will always be beyond reach, strategy for the future always lacks reliable empirical test data. Consider US and NATO options vis-à-vis the assertive geostrategic ambition shown by Vladimir Putin today. We depend upon the practical reality of our dependence upon assumptions that we have and that we believe to be prudent. US and NATO strategy may be sufficiently well chosen to protect against clear and major acts of aggression, but the experience of statecraft and strategy doesn't always play ball by presenting only unambiguous evidence of tolerable or intolerable behaviour. Indeed, statesmen and strategists regard the physical geographical context for their concerns more as a stage set for the play in which they intend to assume a leading role, and also to write the script. This role commands definition of the political stakes at issue. The mighty concepts of grand strategy, geopolitics and geostrategy can be viewed as grand narratives. Such narratives are stories, tales composed, woven and perhaps executed principally as exercises of political will, rather than as faithful reflections of physical realities. I do not dismiss the exercise of imagination and political will as being merely creativity. My purpose, rather, is to claim that the geophysical world calls for reinterpretation and exploitation of what seem to be logically advisable and emotionally compelling options, often leading to action in statecraft.

## Mackinder and Spykman: Ventures in Very Grand Theory

Since the mid twentieth century, theorists of International Relations, even those who have been brave enough to advise governments on high policy and strategy, have been unwilling, or intellectually unable to 'boldly go' – to employ the dubious grammar of *Star Trek* – into the inclusive field of geopolitics and geostrategy. Geopolitics was found guilty by its perceived close association with the imperial ambitions of the Nazi regime.[12] There was some limited merit in this accusation of guilt by association, but the consequence of this politically correct view has been a notable lack of significant political and strategic analysis that takes geography into account. Bearing in mind geopolitical and geostrategic considerations need only mean that one is alert to the possible relevance of geography for political and strategic issues. Both politics and strategy can be influenced significantly by claimed geographical facts and strong opinions about geography, whether or not they are well founded. Although it is true that the concepts behind political and strategic affairs can triumph for a while over objective realities, it is not true to believe – with the Führer – that the human will is capable of ignoring severely adverse practical realities. Global strategic history always has been governed in practice by logistics, meaning the science of supply and movement. As a sweeping generalization, this basically remains as much the case today as it was a century ago. In the most practical of terms concerning the future of strategy, the core focus here is a logistical story. One might think that in the twenty-first century technologies would have resolved the dilemmas and cleared the geophysical obstructions that in the past hampered logistical provision for the projection of military power. But, by and large, this is not so. Supply – including replenishment and repair of damage suffered in combat – and movement have been altered greatly by the arrival of fast-moving trans-oceanic air transport, and by the availability of fairly secure IT on a global basis. However, it would be a great mistake to assume potentially significant logistical challenges no longer matter.

For example, the predictable US–Chinese contest for hegemony on- and offshore the coastal Rimland of Asia–Pacific is dominated strategically by the major asymmetrical facts that the People's Republic of China is itself politically present there, while the United States is not. Although the details have changed, the geostrategic fact remains that, as in the Second World War, the United States requires bases in the Pacific located much farther east than the Hawaiian Islands.[13] Guam in the Mariana Islands looks likely to be as strategically important tomorrow as it was in 1944–5. For another example of physical geographical conditions intruding on strategic calculations, even in this era of global IT and intercontinental missiles that may carry nuclear warheads, consider the geography of Vladimir Putin's dramatic move to re-acquire the Crimean peninsula for Russia. Ukraine, let alone the Crimea, reminds us that strategy is about power projection. If military power cannot be projected into the Black Sea or perhaps the coastal waters around Taiwan, then the political scope for practicable strategic options must be severely limited.

Bearing in mind the importance of logistics for every strategy, it is appropriate to emphasize the significance of geography in strategic thinking. I mentioned above that theorists of International Relations have appeared to be snake-bitten for more than fifty years with respect to the geographical dimension of world affairs. The future of strategy, globally, will be notably influenced by geographical considerations of all kinds. Two very important theorists of world politics and strategy were the British geographer Sir Halford Mackinder (1861–1947) and the Dutch-American social scientist Nicholas John Spykman (1893–1943).[14] The most important reason for citing these two theorists of geopolitics is not so much to suggest the relevance of their ideas to the policy and strategy needs of the future, as to introduce readers to global views worthy of the term. As is often the case with potent theory, the dominant ideas of these two theorists can be expressed and explained quite simply. Indeed, the relative ease of translation of these scholars' reasoning into policy and strategy – as guidelines – often entails dangerously casual quotation and misquotation. A genuinely global political and strategic context is of great importance to our analysis. Mackinder and Spykman shared primary concerns for world order and, therefore, as a prerequisite, for the global balance of power. Their central views were expressed in the form of claimed logical dicta. Sir Halford Mackinder wrote as follows in 1919:

*Who rules East Europe commands the Heartland:*

*Who rules the Heartland commands the World-Island:*

*Who rules the World-Island commands the World.*[15] (italics added for emphasis)

By 'World-Island', Sir Halford was referring to the bi-continent of Eurasia–Africa. By 'the Heartland', he meant that central region in Eurasia where the rivers drain only to inland seas or towards the generally ice-bound Arctic Ocean. In other words, thinking strategically, the Heartland was that region of the world's surface unreachable by seapower. Sir Halford was a British liberal imperialist of late Victorian vintage, and his primary strategic anxiety was always the security of Britain and its empire.[16] Over millennia, in his view, the grandest of protracted strategic competitions had been between landpower and seapower. Although Britain's maritime hegemony was not to be seriously challenged until Imperial Germany launched its High Seas Fleet in the early years of the twentieth century, Mackinder was acutely aware of the fragility of maritime empire in the face of anticipated continental challenge. He realized that a totally maritime-dependent Britain needed both some continental alliance to distract would-be rival landward hegemons, and to ensure that a healthy naval imbalance could be sustained. Sir Halford's nightmare was a vision of German – or, much later, Soviet – continental hegemony, exploited for the strategic purpose of maritime, and therefore global, dominance as well.

Nicholas John Spykman theorized, in some contrast to Mackinder's geopolitical and geostrategic nightmare that would see landpower so dominant in Eurasia, that it might, as a consequence, be able to acquire a dominant seapower in addition. Writing in 1942, only a year before his early death, Spykman provided the following argument, in contrast to that uttered by Mackinder a generation before:

> *Who controls the rimland rules Eurasia;*
>
> *Who rules Eurasia controls the destinies of the world.*[17]
> (italics added for emphasis)

As we can see, both great geopolitical theorists and policy advocates were able to express the core idea in their theories in very simple – even simplistic – terms. The ideas most central to Mackinder and to Spykman were explained with an almost brutal directness, which contrasts with much scholarly analysis. Despite the obvious difference between Mackinder and Spykman, what matters most is the fact that they agreed on the identity of the principal strategic challenge to the polity/ies closest to their hearts and interests. They agreed that, in the future as in the past, potentially lethal danger to the kind of world they favoured would lie in the super-continent of Eurasia–Africa being dominated by a single and therefore inevitably hegemonic power. The two theorists saw it as a fact that the power potential of Eurasia, if controlled by a single state, would in the long run pose a deadly unanswerable challenge to the offshore islands, and even continents, that were British and/or American home territory. However, Spykman departed quite dramatically from Mackinder, in that he believed the inner geographical coastal crescent comprising China, the monsoon lands of Southern Asia, and Europe, harboured greater potential power than did the rather barren Eurasian Heartland identified by Mackinder. This meant that political and strategic menace from the Heartland could be balanced (and more) on-shore in Eurasia, but there could be acute peril if a single power were to unite rimland resources for aggressive purpose.[18]

The principal reason for my introducing the grand geo-political and geostrategic theories of Mackinder and Spykman is not for the sake of detailed argument, because it would be absurd to consider now the future relevance of ideas conceived and developed in the first half of the twentieth century – or would it? What we find is that, if we take away the historically specific detail, both of these great theorists identified problems, and located political and strategic solutions, that are still highly relevant today. The main reasons why this could happen are those high-lighted earlier in this text, though here I would add the enduring potency of geography in its several meanings, physical as well as perceived and interpreted. It should be recalled that I have identified three grand villains that serve all too ably to explain all of Man's grim historical experience. I have found that human nature, the human necessity for political organization and, as a direct result, the need for strategy provide the explanatory ammunition required for laying bare the reasons for our beastly past, present and probably future.

When we slot in the grander ideas of Mackinder and Spykman, we find that the enduring geographical facts so vital to their ideas are still relevant to our enquiry into the future of strategy. By far the most significant difference between the two sets of theories is that Mackinder sees a recurring continental threat from a Heartland peril to the balance of power, whereas Spykman somewhat more optimistically believes that the true power potential of Eurasia lies in its Rimland rather than its Heartland. Moving from geopolitical and geostrategic theory to the real world of political and strategic choice, we discover that only the leading state players and organizers in the twentieth century's balance of world power and international order – Great Britain and, a little later, the United States – appear to have accepted both the political and strategic logic expounded by the great theorists. To cut to the chase with two examples, in 1914–18 the British Empire waged an almost total war to preserve the balance of power and International Order; while, in 1946–9, the United States made the most momentous of political and strategic commitments in order to prevent Soviet control of the Rimland around Eurasia. In both cases, the geostrategic logic was plainly born out of the political meaning attributed to physical geography. Both Britain and the United States reasoned that they could not be safe if there was an unbalanced strategic threat in continental Eurasia.

A geopolitical and geostrategic perspective can provide a key that may unlock what otherwise might be the mysteries of statecraft. In essence, Mackinder and Spykman, along with a few others, enable a clear enough plausible answer to be provided to the greatest of the statesman's and strategist's questions: 'So what?' The practical answer provided by literally centuries of English, then British, and later American, politics and strategy is clear. Because the potential resources of Eurasia are so great, it must always be balanced, if not over-compensated, lest it achieves a global dominance. Having an offshore (Eurasian) location was recognized as providing some security, but technological developments do not permit a relaxed attitude towards threats from the continental East, in Eurasia. In 1740, for example, Horace Walpole, son of British Prime Minister Robert Walpole, observed that 'if there is no diversion by a land war upon the continent and we have no security against invasion from France besides our own strength, I am afraid that by next spring or summer the seat of war will be in this island'.[19]

Now we must turn to the relative significance of strategies that rely principally upon the now traditional strengths associated with the land, sea and air environments, respectively. Reliable commentary on the strategic meaning of cyberpower is notably lacking at present.[20]

## Strategies are Joint

As a general rule throughout strategic history, landpower and seapower have been more or less interdependent. That said, it can also be claimed that particular security communities have usually favoured either a mainly maritime, or a principally continental landpower orientation in their military power and hence in their preference for strategy. While it is true – if somewhat banal – to maintain that every war is different, we mustn't accept that fact blindly. Military power at all times and of all kinds is united in its function and dynamics.[21] This claim supports the thesis that strategy, regarded functionally, is not a modern discovery. However, no matter how much different conflicts may have in common, in principle, it is an enduring fact of strategic history that qualitatively different kinds of military power work in different ways and succeed or fail for reasons that are quite distinctive. Most of strategic history reveals relatively clearly the sense of mutual need that binds landpower and seapower together. In the twentieth century, the military and strategic complications added by airpower, spacepower, cyberpower and – arguably (as an effectively independent element) – nuclear weapons increased the burdens as well as the exploitable opportunities, in 'mixing and matching' complementary components of military power from physically distinctive geographies.

It is very much the case today, when considering the future of strategy, that the larger and potentially more powerful states each have tendencies in military focus that are largely due to national geography, especially with respect to location, the stage-set for strategic experience. Of course, there are many reasons why a particular polity maintains, for example, a maritime-oriented military establishment. But the enduring geographical setting, and probably a historical feeling of greater or lesser insecurity, affect the choice of strategic focus. It is important to note, however, that an exclusive strategic orientation which places too much emphasis on military strength geared for a specific geography – land, sea or air, in particular – can prove woefully vulnerable if strategic history takes an unanticipated course. Had Germany been able to employ submarines correctly and in large numbers, victory over Britain and her allies might well have been won in 1917.

It is important to recognize that each geographically specialized form of military power is vitally important, both in itself as a contributor to strategic effect, and as an enabling factor for other contributing agents. For example, in the 1990s, allied airpower destroyed Iraqi air defences comprehensively, a fact that both freed up real-time air assault assistance to friendly ground forces, and removed Iraqi ability to intervene from the air in the (very limited) fighting on the ground. There have been phases in conflicts for which airpower was relatively insignificant, but this has been the exception since early in the Second World War.

Since the late 1930s it has been quite common for any one of landpower, seapower or airpower to be regarded and employed as the lead element in planned and executed war making. Inevitably, inter-service rivalries and advocacy of new technology will claim that 'all we need is' the army, the navy or the air force, because the most favoured service can be augmented organically – say, with helicopters and short- and medium-range missiles. Each geographically specialized kind of military power can be employed, though not usually to greatest effect, for non-traditional functions. However, the distinctive physical geographies behind the separate armed services are heavily laden with a unique logic of strategic effect and, indeed, with a distinctive culture that cannot easily be acquired elsewhere and should not be casually ignored.[22]

Although landpower, seapower and airpower can each serve usefully in support, and sometimes even in place, of the others, nonetheless there is a core strategic meaning and value to each geographical military specialization. *Landpower*, or 'boots on the ground', is essentially intended to be about physical control of terrestrial happenings. *Seapower* is all about communications, because that is the way that mankind most usefully can exploit such a large environment. Since we cannot live at sea, we have to consider seapower principally in the context of (near-global) mobility. *Airpower* has several major strategic roles, including mobility, but, regarded strategically, it is uniquely capable of reaching out swiftly over great distances to deliver hurt from above. Seapower and airpower as the leading edge of strategy share the advantage of requiring only minimum risk to human life on the ground. This is advantageous in terms of risk reduction to friendly forces, but it can be an important negative when viewed as a display to the enemy of commitment to deter. Regarded overall, both landpower and seapower these days include organic elements of airpower, while the strategic contexts of focus for seapower and airpower have usually been found to require assistance from landpower in order to secure physical terrestrial control.

Bearing in mind that we humans can live only upon the land, it is obvious that more often than not the strategic effect required by policy is some physical evidence of map-locatable political control on the ground. One must never forget that strategy is always an instrument of policy and politics, and that it is not *about* combat per se. Armed conflict – war and warfare – is really only about the consequences of the violence that is organized and applied. In order to exploit military success or advantage, it is usual for the winning side to insist upon some friendly local presence on the ground, mainly to ensure that the price paid by its soldiers is not lost in the political turmoil that tends to follow warfare. Winning the war, but losing the peace, is a familiar description of the historical record of strategy in action.

When countries and alliances decide to fight, they need to remember that the way they choose to wage war, meaning the strategy/ies they pursue, assuredly will leave a legacy on the ground in the kind of post-war order established. A war won by missile strikes from over the horizon, possibly from tens of thousands of feet up, or from mobile forces that, being nearly always at sea, have had no direct impact on the enemy's population, will not have had any opportunity to contribute usefully to a post-war political order. This is not to demean the use of military power, because that power remains essential as a tool of order. However, it is important to remember that choices between strategies are very likely to have quite long-lasting consequences, for good or ill.

The final chapter here accepts two critically important challenges. First, I shall endeavour to explain the differences that nuclear weapons have or have not made for statecraft and strategy, while second I shall draw together the key arguments and assertions made in this book to draw out what they tell us about the future of strategy.

# – 6 –

# Strategy and the Future

Fortunately for my confidence in the argument in this text, but unfortunately for my aspirations for the future of the human race, I am convinced that our collective future will be essentially the same as it has been and is in the past and present. This is not, at least not necessarily, a pessimistic conclusion. Although the history of our species has been notably bloody, one is compelled by the historical record to conclude that it could have been a great deal worse – though it could still turn out to be so! The story line carried by this text is one of tolerably successful management. There has been no end in sight to the unpleasant reality of strategic peril, a political condition that continues to this day. As best we can tell from the evidence available to us, Mankind has always been challenged, both by natural causes and by persisting problems of collective governance. The mere facts that a book on *The Future of Strategy* can be written and is deemed worthy of publication today are themselves hopeful signs: it is encouraging to think that we will have need for strategy in the future.

On a personal note, I have studied and debated strategy for fifty years, ten of which were in the security context of fairly acute interstate tension in the later stages of the Cold War. More to the point, I have both worked on the theory and contributed to the official practice of nuclear strategy for many years. I mention this to provide some evidence in support of the argument of this book. My belief that there is and will be substantial continuity in the strategic dimension of the human future, does not, I believe, mean that I am complacent about potential dangers. This whole narrative of strategic concerns really amounts to a record in the management of peril. I argue that neither strategy in general, nor nuclear strategy in particular, can usefully or hopefully be regarded as a problem (or problems). As a general rule, problems can be regarded either as solvable or at least as capable of improvement. The evidence of our continuous strategic history suggests strongly that the security problems we continue to face can neither be solved nor convincingly alleviated. However, there is good reason, based on historical experience, to believe that, collectively, we will be able politically to manage reasonably well the undoubted dangers that we face as a result of our all too human urges, anxieties and even motivations.

In this concluding chapter, I attempt to confront nuclear danger frankly and realistically, and to relate its consequences to the main thread of argument in this book. While granting the persistent peril of possible nuclear use, the narrative here concludes by summarizing the whole argument of the preceding text. My conclusion has to be a mixed one. The future of strategy must be shaped and driven by our political life, and that causal chain reaches back to our human nature. Strategy is an important part of the human political solution to the endless quest for tolerable security; it is a story without a conclusion. The argument here is also strongly supportive of the outstanding analysis and argument in Christopher Coker's recent book *Can War be Eliminated?*[1]

## The Nuclear Exception?

There are many reasons why strategies fail to deliver what their authors intended and possibly even promised politically, but there is only one game-changing strategic cloud permanently in the sky of world politics – nuclear weapons.[2] These weapons are uniquely capable of causing fatal, irreversible harm to otherwise possibly prudent intentions. That said, there are unfortunately no prospects of nuclear threat – latent or actual – being removed from our future. Readers should appreciate that the invention and development of nuclear weaponry did not happen just by chance. The weaponization of atomic fission was the cumulatively inevitable consequence of more than a century of dedicated and highly competent, yet innovative, labour by world-class pure and applied scientists from more than a dozen branches of science and engineering.[3] More to the point, what became known as the Manhattan Project (of 1942–5) was fuelled and driven by exactly those fundamental enduring motivations that I have cited throughout this text, inspired by Thucydides' *History of the Peloponnesian War* – fear, honour and interest. These need to be added to a brew of human nature, political organization and, finally, the structure and logic of strategy. It should be plain to see that nuclear weapons are unlikely to be categorized anytime soon as simply another type of weapon, having much fundamentally in common with the other weapons in human arsenals.

I single out nuclear weapons because they are radically different from all other weapons, in their nature and, as a consequence, in their potential strategic effect. This difference is so great that it poses the sole fundamental challenge to the potential integrity of the structure and working of strategy in the future. I should probably mention I specialized for nearly twenty years in strategic issues dominated by nuclear weapons. It is ironic that, in a book that takes a positive view of strategy in the human future, I am obliged to endorse the idea that nuclear weapons simultaneously both endanger and enable the strategy function. This may not seem an adequate position for an author to take, but a lifetime of study and some first-hand participation in nuclear issues in several countries have led me to believe the following:

1. Nuclear weapons are uniquely different from other weapons. They can be so powerful and wide-ranging in the devastation they can cause that the entire structure of the strategy project – with its (political) ends, (strategic) ways and (military) means – would not be able to function meaningfully. So much damage would be wrought that no sane (let alone political) ends would be served by nuclear use.

2. Although it is (just, possibly) feasible to imagine and plan for the very limited employment of nuclear weapons in war, the risks of escalation in the competitive confusion of nuclear conflict would certainly be terrifyingly high.[4] Political and strategic paralysis caused by fear, no matter how understandable in advance and likely in practice, can provide only an uncomfortable basis upon which to sustain international order. After all, accidents can and do happen. The expectation of care in political decision making cannot be taken for granted. Flawed human beings can never be entirely trusted to be reasonable, rational and prudent – certainly not by the 'other side' in a conflict.

3. The discovery of nuclear power and then the rapid move to weaponization can be likened to Pandora's Box – once opened, it can never be closed. We humans are stuck with nuclear weapons, if for no better reason than that they cannot be abolished. We cannot disarm ourselves of the relevant enabling scientific discoveries;

we know why and how atoms can be split, and also, how they can be made to fuse. It follows, then, that nuclear peril needs to be carefully controlled strategically, if we accept nuclear weapons can never be abolished. If some readers are understandably inclined to accept any variant of a 'Project Zero' that would eliminate nuclear weapons, all I can say, with regret, is that the historical record of arms control and disarmament is deeply unimpressive.[5] Given the extraordinarily high value commonly attributed to nuclear armament, it is easy to understand why nuclear abolition would be extremely difficult to achieve.

4. In practice what has happened is that a handful of countries, both large and small (the USA, Russia, the Chinese Peoples' Republic, Britain, France, Israel and North Korea) have sought to make strategic sense of these weapons in varying forms (long- and shorter-range, air-breathing or missile-delivered, and so forth). For almost two decades my primary professional concern was to devise and seek to improve US strategy for the threat or use of these weapons. Few, if any, of the world's strategists can fail to recognize the nature and size of hazard posed by the nuclear context. What we know for certain is that for the seventy years since 1945 no polity has been willing to resort to employment of a nuclear strategy. But we do not fully understand what to make of that incontestable fact. Is it powerful evidence of the controllability, or rather of fears over the possible uncontrollability, of nuclear weapons? A key problem is that the absence of evidence means that there is no support for the proposition that these weapons have not been useful.[6] The challenge of absent evidence permeates the abundant speculation about nuclear strategy. It is extremely difficult to find reliable evidence on human – including political-institutional – motivation and decision. The literature on Strategic Studies, especially on the concept

of deterrence, is well stocked with circumstantial argument pressing the merit in nuclear weapons that is claimed in theory. Claims for deterrence tend to have at their core assumptions and assertions, the kernel of which can be expressed as 'It stands to reason...'. This difficulty with proof of deterrence is not unique to the nuclear context, but it has been exceptionally prominent as a potential weakness in that region of policy and strategy. The main reason there is no evidence regarding nuclear weapons after seventy years persists in this subject. Common sense is all very well, but a phrase such as the 'calculus of deterrence' encourages, if it does not actually license, a dangerously erroneous view of nuclear weapons. The logical structure of mutual nuclear deterrence is easy to grasp. But mutual real-world behaviour that directly and indirectly affects the prospects for successful deterrence is often far removed from the mathematical realm of calculus. The prudent reasons why deterrence ought to hold tend to be dominant on most occasions, but the uncomfortable fact remains that successful mutual deterrence can never be guaranteed. There is a short-list of major reasons why deterrence, even nuclear deterrence, has to be less than certain: these reasons include miscalculation, an unexpected and probably unmanageable chain of events, and also the unexpected strength of human resilience in the face of attempted (nuclear) coercion.

Seventy years into the nuclear age, it remains a strategically embarrassing fact that we cannot, perhaps dare not, place much faith in strategy involving nuclear weapons. They are indispensable because the threat and use of such weapons can only be deterred, or if need be answered appropriately, by military action also of a nuclear kind. The real problem with nuclear weapons is that the impracticality of thoroughly reliable defence makes their use potentially suicidal, when both sides possess nuclear weapons. It would be hard to overstate the scale of this challenge. Western democracies would need to overcome immense difficulties if they were ever to consider seriously the possible use of nuclear weapons. This fact is widely known, but pure abstract logic, as well as actual physical military reality, demand that we retain nuclear arsenals. Today, it is difficult to devise war plans that would yield strategic advantage from using nuclear weapons, while it is easy indeed to design plans for nuclear threat and action that would be just as likely to paralyse us, as to alarm and frustrate an adversary.

I hesitate to write this apparently contradictory thought, but there is no appropriate view of nuclear weapons that one could adopt which would not make unreasonable demands upon our polity, and yet there is no sensible alternative to having them.[7] Science, technology, politics and strategy in malign combination have bequeathed a challenge to strategy that we are unable to meet satisfactorily. An important lesson to be drawn from our history has to be the need to tolerate deeply unwelcome strategic facts. The fact that we are unable to make sensible strategic decisions about nuclear weapons is simply a persisting feature of human existence. There is pathetic irony in the fact that we have been unable to tame the menace in nuclear armaments, and indeed are unlikely to in the future. It is wise for us to attempt to ensure political control and limitation of the use of nuclear weapons in war, but even so a catastrophe is likely to remain possible, or even probable. We are victims of our own success in the attempt to manage security.

Looking to an open-ended future, it is necessary to argue both that strategy will provide a vital tool-set for survival and security, but also that there will continue to be a level of safety that we will not reach reliably concerning the nuclear threat. The awesome nuclear danger that may underpin the stability of international order also constitutes the most deadly of dangers to that order. Though

I choose to be optimistic about the likelihood of our conducting world politics without an active nuclear dimension to acute crises, there are grounds for anxiety, if not alarm. The theory of strategy is unlikely to be able to cope with the persisting peril in the fact that nuclear weapons offer a lethal challenge to the needed overall integrity that renders ends, ways and means such a logically satisfying and neat concept. Having made some modest contribution to nuclear strategy (lore, at least) for many years, I am far from content with this view. I am obliged to argue that, despite its extensive merit, the theory of strategy would almost certainly be of no use if nuclear weapons were to be employed in an actual war. I suggested earlier that conflict and war typically have an almost organic quality that defies prediction. This means that the danger of escalation could be extreme and chaotic, if a war grew in quality and quantity of violence. The future is open-ended. We need to recognize this fact as we contemplate the future of strategy. It is not strategy's fault that its theory cannot control large-scale nuclear hazard reliably. Although I have chosen to identify large-scale nuclear use as a strategic practice certain to threaten the integrity of strategic reasoning – since (strategic) ways and (military) means in effect would destroy (political) ends – it is only an extreme example of a common phenomenon in strategic history. Specifically, extreme expenditure of a polity's effort in the conduct of war is certain to threaten to devour its own (policy) ends. The First World War is an example of a conflict that proved so exhausting to conduct that the warfare served itself as much as – or more than – it advanced polities' ends; indeed, some principal polities literally ceased to exist!

Nuclear weapons will remain essential to the structure and functioning of international order, and even to the apparent stability of a robust balance of power, even though they pose a potentially lethal danger to our future. By their use, the concept of strategic history would be tested beyond likely tolerance and achievable recovery. Unfortunately, no dependable solutions to the nuclear threat can be anticipated in future strategic history.[8] Among the more important messages here is my claim that strategic history has no anticipatable end-point. Some people have difficulty accepting this indeterminate quality to existence.

# Conclusion: What Do We Know with High Confidence?

This book may appear unusual because it has sought to identify what is knowable with high confidence about strategy in our future. I sought to explain in a recent text the ironic balance between our knowledge of the future and our profound ignorance.[1] The apparently asymmetric relationship between the known and the unknown about the strategic future can be classed as ironic, because it is the nature of our knowledge of the future that enables it to be anticipated with confidence. On the one hand, we do not know, and cannot reliably predict by whom, when, what or how deeds laden with strategic meaning will be committed in the twenty-first century. But, on the other hand, we do have highly variable, but still often usable, understanding of what was done or attempted with strategy over the course of 2,500 years! Although knowledge of past deeds and misdeeds cannot provide a reliable guide to future happenings, it certainly can and should serve as evidence of the consequences that often follow from the kind of activities in which security communities choose to engage. This argument leads unavoidably to the conclusion that, although we do not and cannot know in advance who will try to do what, when, where, how or to whom, nonetheless we should be able to anticipate the kind of strategic behaviour that is likely to occur in the future.

Keeping ambitions modest is sensible, because the future of strategy needs understanding in the context of possibilities that we need to be prepared for. Despite the continuing arguments about nuclear strategy, a general alertness to the possibility of nuclear use has to mean that we should prepare for – indeed against – that grim possibility. The use of strategic theory in the control of strategic choice should override anxieties about the fatal possibilities that could arise from nuclear warfare conducted on a large scale. We are too late to avoid the discovery and development of nuclear weapons, and the human political context always has an active need for strategy. It follows that we are left with a probably eternal threat of nuclear danger on a scale that might prevent the functioning of a strategy process.[2] Theory on the waging of limited nuclear war is not very convincing, but it is all we have to help us navigate the military reality of bilateral nuclear war, something we have never experienced before. What we do know is that the unique challenge to the integrity of strategy posed by possible nuclear use cannot sensibly be used to argue against all strategic phenomena. There is far more to strategy than the need for control of nuclear warfare, critically important though that is. The fact that we can conceive of contexts of nuclear use in which devastation cannot be controlled, therefore, is not a good enough reason to be critical of strategic theory. Strategists would do their best to prevent nuclear use from halting the working of strategy, because uncontrollable nuclear war would make a mockery of the very idea and practice of strategy. However, such a war must not bring a premature end to creative thought about how to stop a headlong rush into probable global catastrophe.

I now present four claims that combine to explain the future of strategy.

1. *The need for strategy arises from the enduring nature of the human condition.* This need is ongoing; it can

be ignored and neglected, just as it can be – and often is – performed extremely poorly, but it cannot be abolished. The interdependent concepts that form the key argument about the relevance of the strategy function are not optional; there is no avoiding the importance of (political) ends, (strategic) ways and (military) means – all influenced more or less severely by the prevalence of assumptions best regarded as culturally derived. Decisions about strategic choice and the sheer detail in much of the typical argument about it can obscure clarity of understanding about the phenomenon. Just because there are few learned texts about strategy, and despite the silence that can greet attempts to debate strategy in public, it does not necessarily follow that strategic argument is inaccessible to the amateur. In fact, the basic general structure of strategic theory is simple. After all, how much of a mental challenge is it to grasp these basic interdependent points:

(political) *ends* are the purpose of the endeavour;
(strategic) *ways* choose and specify how the (political) ends should be secured;
(military) *means* are the tactical agents that must be employed in order to have operational consequences with the necessary strategic value; and
*assumptions* are always likely to be crucially important for action contemplated in the future, since reliable empirical evidence about the consequences of future behaviour is certain to be missing at strategy selection time.

The structural conceptual authority of the four ideas just cited and explained is beyond dispute. The interdependencies among the ideas are overwhelming.

2. *The need for strategy is the product of human nature, just as its realization must take forms that are political.* A few historians have sought to argue, unpersuasively, that understanding of strategy is a relatively recent historical development, traceable back with any

certainty only to the 1770s. Because strategy is a concept rather than something material, many people have difficulty understanding what it really means.[3] Also, the use of the concept of strategy seemingly by any- and everybody, and its alleged relevance to realms far removed from the military, mean that there are few limits to the behaviours and even objects that claim to be strategic. As an idea, strategy at its core is about consequences, rather than about some quantity or quality in itself. When historians refer to the strategic bridge over the lower Rhine at Arnhem, what they mean to do is to highlight the importance of the bridge in September 1944, given the wartime context of a near-complete absence of intact bridges over the principal river that Allied forces needed to cross in order to complete the defeat of German forces in the West. We label as strategic particular objectives for our planned behaviour, simply because of their importance assessed in terms of the consequences we believe could follow from their achievement. Strategic significance is typically attributed because of the flow of events, not the innate properties of some man-made or natural geographical features. In 1914 and again in 1917, the village of Passchendaele on a low ridge north of the small town of Ypres, was assigned strategic importance in the First World War. Retention of Ypres was significant for the security of the Channel ports that were vital to the logistical lifeline of the British Expeditionary Force (BEF) between Flanders and England. Allied holding of Ypres posed a constant, if frequently dormant, menace to Germany's rail-bound logistics in the Low Countries. The strategic meaning of both natural and man-made geography can be acquired more by the circumstances of conflict than is revealed even by careful study. In the Second World War, the German sieges of Sevastopol in the Crimea in 1942, and the Soviet holding of Stalingrad on the Volga late in 1942 into early 1943, were both substantively important, but nonetheless were probably of even greater significance due to the political meaning attributed to them. While the structural architecture of strategy is the product of a human nature obliged to think in terms of ends, ways and means, the attribution of strategic meaning to the agencies for threat and action will be largely optional. Strategy has to serve politics, and must always have political consequences, but the rationality of the choices made and implemented can, and often does, warrant criticism. The bare abstract theory of strategy serves only to organize a world that needs to relate (political) ends to (military) ways and means, but such logical interdependency offers no guarantee of success in planning or subsequent action. Strategic theory, particularly of an austere general kind, contributes to the education of those required to think strategically; it cannot and certainly does not itself ensure that 'strategic' decisions will be either soundly conceived or carefully put into action. When there is public disagreement over strategy, there is no sense in challenging the concept of strategy per se, because the basic architecture of that idea is applied empty of specific content to argument that will be settled by very human individuals and groups acting within and through political process. Of course, there are other essential details of all kinds that have to be managed, ranging from efforts to reduce risks to logistical provision, but every strategic project, great or small, is shaped, driven and ultimately judged strategically with reference to politics.

3. *The character, but not the nature, of strategy alters with circumstances of perceived need.* Much writing about strategy suffers from the counterproductive influence of the false belief that strategy per se changes in order to accommodate new situations and challenges. Also, the concept of revolution is frequently used to convey understanding of the significance of

change. The widespread confusion about change and continuity is easily resolved once one recognizes the essential distinction between strategy's character and its nature.

The general theory of strategy is unchanging, except in the details that change to match contemporary attitudes and, naturally, for translation across cultural frontiers. The reason I insist on carefully defining this change and continuity is to ensure that the enduring truth in general theory is not lost in dealing with the needs of the moment. Action in pursuit of policy always requires assistance in the form of behaviour guided by strategy. The variable character of political objectives will be met by suitably specialized military acts geared to meet particular circumstances. But the course of strategic history is not, and cannot be, matched by almost automatic shifts in the logic of strategy, marching as in locked-step. The relationships among ends, ways and means alter with cultural, technological and social changes, but fundamental interdependencies still hold, even when adapted to contemporary realities. For example, the early years of the Second World War required large-scale adaptation and adjustment among the different forms of military power, as states strove to compete effectively in a context of universal learning in the real-time of war. The vital point is the proposition that strategic thought and practice do not alter, even though they have to be realized in the military detail most appropriate to time, place and circumstances. When professional historians complain that social scientists steal ruthlessly and anachronistically from the historical episodes that appear best to suit their arguments, they can indeed be right. That said, it does not follow that a greater appreciation of the local detail of a time long past will necessarily lead to misunderstanding of the thought process behind decisions that were taken then. If the Ancients – as well as those of more recent vintage – were obliged by political,

military and other circumstances to provide answers
that then made current sense to the challenge by seeking
compatible interdependencies among ends, ways and
means, we can say that they functioned strategically. It
does not matter for the integrity of theory what contemporary detail was inserted into the three categories.
It matters not at all for the authority of theory which
assumptions historical figures employed about their
world, because it is the functioning of the trio of interdependent organizing concepts that is important, not
the detail of their contemporary historical content.
Historians can have difficulty understanding this argument.[4] In effect, I am claiming that ancient thought
and practice illustrates change from, but also continuity with, today. We humans should be understood as
thinking and behaving strategically whether we are
armed with a *gladius* and *pilum* or with a missile-firing
aerial drone. Strategy is strategy, regardless of the realities of tactical change or even revolution. Strategy
therefore is subject to almost constant change as the
political demands upon it alter over time, but also
needs to be understood as a permanent political function that does not change its nature from one period
to another.

4. *There is no final solution to the challenge posed by
   strategic requirements and occasional dilemmas.* Strategy is beyond definitive reform and cannot be eliminated, no matter how sincerely and intensely some
   among us might wish otherwise. The future of strategy
   has to be seen and understood as nesting in a great and
   hopefully unending stream of time. It had no historical
   beginning in any way accessible to us, and most likely
   it will have no end in the future, unless we inflict terminal harm on our physical and political condition as
   a result of the mishandling of the nuclear challenge.
   There may be other menaces prospectively lethal to
   *Homo sapiens* – e.g. intervention by hostile aliens, an

asteroid strike or fatal climate change – but at this time of writing, only nuclear peril can be cited as a possibly terminal threat that we ourselves have created. Our education and political system are so geared to thinking in terms of periods that it is not easy to cope intellectually with the possibility of an endlessly strategic future. If readers examine closely their favourite works on the human political condition, they are likely to discover that the preferred authors rest their leading arguments on only implicit assumptions about where we are heading in political organization. Fanciful futures radically different from today are not hard to invent, but as a seriously intended venture of the imagination, such futures are not worth the electricity and printer ink they command. The future is so uncertain that it is hardly worthy of serious commitment of scarce time and resources today. The future security context of human political communities is sure to need strategy; this has been the case for all of our species' history to date, so why would it change for the future? An obvious answer could lie in the genuinely lethal novelty of a possible nuclear catastrophe, but even with such a dire notion in mind, one has to recognize that the human race has functioned politically, and strategically, despite nearly seventy years of nuclear danger already. Even if one can argue persuasively that radical political or cultural change is needed urgently, it is not easy to conceive of likely circumstances that would lead to a genuinely post-nuclear world.

## Strategy and the 'Great Stream of Time'

On balance, should one be pessimistic or optimistic about the future of strategy in human affairs? It is all too easy to be weighed down by the grim possibility that a nuclear conflict beyond rational strategic control might mar this new century and threaten to end the history of our species. We think we know how to control and minimize the dangers of a nuclear holocaust occurring, but there are still ample grounds to be afraid. In this short book I have identified and developed three possible reasons for alarm: (1) human nature and its unchanging sources of motivation; (2) political organization into security communities; and (3) the unavoidable necessity for strategic thought and behaviour. These three features that have persisted throughout human history need to be appreciated as enduring facts supported by an incontrovertible weight of evidence: they are not high and abstract theory, they are the continuing record in history of our species' deeds and misdeeds.

However, all is by no means lost in the legacy from the past to the future that is my primary focus here. The proposition that strategy has a secure future does not require energetic argument, because it can be shown clearly to provide a service that is always needed. We do not need to be taught to consider the world in terms of the ends that we desire, and the ways and means for gaining them. It is all but inconceivable to approach problems in any other way. The difficulty historically has not been in understanding how best to approach a policy challenge, but in the political choices made, and the perennial difficulty of knowing, or usually guessing, which military means, employed in which ways, are likely to succeed at bearable societal cost in the unique context of contemporary challenge.

Despite the certainty (barring the nuclear catastrophe mentioned earlier) that the need for prudent strategic performance is permanent, we cannot avoid noticing that our society and its political leaders do not appear to inhabit, and behave on behalf of, a long-term future. The great stream of time is a potent concept, but it lacks executive authority.[5] Neither politicians nor their electorates consider a future much beyond the ambitious reach even of a rather bold calendar. There are some excellent reasons why the future is a concept typically beyond our grasp. To risk stating the obvious, it is important to understand – really understand – that, by definition, the future never comes. We can only live in the present. The concept of a great stream of time has the potential to mislead as well as to provide useful historical context. Specifically, it is no easy task to manage the necessary fusion in understanding needed to grasp the grand ideas of continuity in change, and change in continuity. There is no doubt that there has to be a future for strategy, but there is uncertainty over whether the human race will behave politically with the necessary caution concerning weapons of mass destruction to enable that future. The concept of the great stream of time encourages a healthy respect for the past, because it is a metaphor with content that promotes understanding of why the future must be made of material, processed in an ever-dynamic today, but largely inherited from yesterday. As Karl Marx warned, we may make future history continuously, but we are condemned to make and remake it with materials provided by yesterday and today.[6] Strategy in the future will be generated and applied to fit with perceived need; but that strategy will be near identical in its functions and purposes to the strategy of the past and present. Strategic history has been made in all times and in all circumstances. Human social life is as unimaginable without a strategic theme as it would be without the pervasive motives in Thucydides' triptych of fear, honour and interest, and denied the comforts of politics. It is most appropriate to consider the future of strategy, the need for politics, and the persistence of human motivation as a single holistic bundle that cannot be disentangled from each other. The stream of time provides the most suitable metaphorical context for this discussion. A major challenge to statecraft and strategy is the difficulty of proposing for an ever-changing today, with no idea of its shelf-life. The temptation to mortgage the long- and even the medium-term future in the interest of anticipated short-term advantage can be seen as permanent. Strategy is here

to stay! The endlessly binary nature of change and continuity that is our history means that the most enduring
function of strategy is management of potentially lethal
dangers. Strategies need to be 'right enough' to enable us
to survive the perils of today, ready – and possibly able –
to cope strategically with the crises of tomorrow.

# Further Reading

Given that the purpose of *The Future of Strategy* is to consider the fundamentals of the subject over the long term, I decided to exercise serious self-discipline and suggest only the very best of books that should be used in strategic education. The candidates' list for potential inclusion was, unsurprisingly, very lengthy. The approach to strategy taken in this book did not lend itself to dividing the reading list by chapters, so I decided to suggest further reading confined to a short list of authors who have addressed the whole subject of strategy. The list here contains only seventeen books from six countries/cultures, with eleven books written in the past 2,400 years, though mainly, I admit, since the 1820s.

I must begin by suggesting that readers acquire some familiarity with three authors who I believe have written what should be regarded as the classical canon on strategy: these authors, Carl von Clausewitz, Sun Tzu and Thucydides, of course, were respectively Prussian/German, Chinese and Greek/Athenian. First, in order of merit in theorization, Clausewitz, *On War*, trans. Michael Howard and Peter Paret (1832–4; Princeton: Princeton University Press, 1976), has no equals. The book is dense and somewhat unfinished, but it provides more plausible and even subtle explanation than can be found in a library of books by lesser authors. Next comes Sun Tzu, *The Art of War*, trans. Samuel B. Griffith (Oxford: Clarendon Press, 1963). This short work is far more subtle than it appears to be in its presentation-like form. While concentrating in the main on generalship, it does have much of value to say about political statecraft. My third entry for the classic canon – Thucydides, *The Landmark Thucydides: A Comprehensive Guide to 'The Peloponnesian War'*, ed. Robert B. Strassler, rev. trans. Richard Crawley (*c*.455–400 BC; New York: The Free Press, 1996) – is a work on statecraft of truly timeless value. Although there is much on war in this book, there is even more on high and low politics. Much in Thucydides rings true for today as well as for Greek inter-city politics in the late fifth century BC. The book is a little biased, as some scholars today enjoy telling us, but that is scarcely an insightful appreciation.

Beyond the 'canon', I recommend giving high priority to eight books in particular. First, I endorse Edward N. Luttwak, *Strategy: The Logic of War and Peace*, rev. edn (Cambridge, MA: Belknap Press of Harvard University Press, 2001). This is a characteristically bold work, respectful but not slavish towards the canon I have cited already. Luttwak is pleasingly comprehensive in his treatment of strategy and war, and he is alert to the reasons for lack of cohesion among politics, strategy, operations and tactics. Next I am pleased to praise J. C. Wylie (USN), *Military Strategy: A General Theory of Power Control* (1967; Annapolis, MD: Naval Institute Press, 1989). This book is very modest in length, but is almost overflowing with pertinent insight. Wylie's observations on types of strategies and on the goal of achieving control over the enemy are both excellent. Probably even more important is the authority he brings to the robust argument that 'the man on the scene with a gun' (i.e., the soldier) is in real control. This modest work on crisis and war also contains some extremely convincing brief characterizations of rival armed services' military cultures. This is truly a small gem of theory – based on practice more than most! Moving on, Beatrice Heuser, *The Evolution of Strategy: Thinking War from Antiquity to the Present* (Cambridge: Cambridge University Press, 2010), is a unique, deeply researched and digested, history of strategic thought. This is a book for which we have been waiting. It is well written, with ample obscure references, and makes a generally successful effort to grasp movements in thought in relation to attempted strategic practice. This is, however, a history of theory and not a history of strategy in action. Heuser does shed much light on the thought behind strategic behaviour and mis-behaviour. This is a genuinely major work of scholarship, reflecting keen skills in theory dissection and a telling eye for sociological context. The exceedingly large library of relatively recent works on nuclear strategy and closely related matters contains no finer work than Bernard Brodie, *War and Politics* (New York: Macmillan, 1973). Brodie was the most perceptive among the school of nuclear-age theorists and analysts in the United States. His work was often profound, and usually – though not invari-ably – well balanced. He was a social scientist by training, but actually more of a historian by inclination. His, typi-cally, was the most sensible sounding voice amidst the intellectual uproar at the RAND Corporation in the 1950s. This book, which is really a collection of separate analyses, contains much that is uniquely insightful and certainly sets the record straight regarding the intellectual fads and fash-ions of the United States in the 1960s. For first-hand insight into the relations among strategic thinking, strate-gic practice and the politics of policy, *War and Politics* has few equals. Brodie was a man of long experience and wide reading, and it shows.

Adding to the short list here, though rather immodestly, I wish to suggest one of my own books, *The Strategy Bridge: Theory for Practice* (Oxford: Oxford University Press, 2010). In this work, I sought to present a general theory of strategy and also to consider the value of theory to those who must decide and command strategy in the real world. Whether or not I succeeded is a matter of judgement I must leave to my readers. I do insist, though, that I helped to draw attention to needed debate and understanding on such vital topics as the difficulties that beset strategists, and the meaning of the strategist's product, the rather mysterious 'strategic effect'! *The Strategy Bridge* is the first book in my strategy trilogy with Oxford University Press, the second and third books being *Perspectives on Strategy* (2013) and *Strategy and Defence Planning* (2014).

Now I need to mention a book that is extremely helpful especially, but certainly not exclusively, for students: Thomas M. Kane, *Strategy: Key Thinkers* (Cambridge: Polity, 2013). Kane's perceptive book offers both insightful commentaries on the works on strategy by 'key thinkers' – as the title promises – and deep understanding of the subject. Kane provides philosophical, historical and some real-world context, in his unravelling of the merit in some strategic ideas. As a work on the theory and practice of strategy throughout history, this modest book has rarely been bettered. This is a first-rate introduction (and more!) to our subject. Next, I recommend reading two books with Williamson Murray as the leading editor: Murray, MacGregor Knox and Alvin Bernstein, eds., *The Making of Strategy: Rulers, States, and War* (Cambridge: Cambridge University Press, 1994), and Murray and Richard Hart Sinnreich, eds., *Successful Strategies: Triumphing in War and Peace from Antiquity to the Present* (Cambridge: Cambridge University Press, 2014). These collections of major original studies covering millennia of history are invaluable sources of careful opinion on strategies in practice through the ages.

Last, but assuredly not least, I must recommend two books by the doyen of British strategic thinkers and commenters, Sir Michael Howard. In a series of volumes of his lectures, he has offered an unrivalled collection of wise thoughts on strategy. The two of his books I recommend here are *The Causes of Wars and Other Essays* (London: Counterpoint, 1984) and *The Lessons of History* (New Haven, CT: Yale University Press, 1991). Readers will find intellectual gems on strategy in history throughout both of these glittering works. For example, they will discover that 'history . . . teaches no lessons' (*Lessons*, 11), and that military history needs to be studied and understood in 'width', 'depth', and 'context'. Memorable and useful aphorisms pepper these lively pages.

I conclude this short list by advising, first, the reading of Christopher Coker, *Can War be Eliminated?* (Cambridge: Polity, 2014). Coker's negative answer to the question he sets himself is, alas, thoroughly persuasive. My short book on *The Future of Strategy* may well make more sense to possibly sceptical readers in the context of the argument provided in lively style by Coker. Second, I shall risk appearing to go off-piste by citing my liking for Aleksandr A. Svechin, *Strategy*, 2nd edn. (1927; Minneapolis, MIN: East View Information Services, 1992). In some parts, this book is worthy of comparison with Clausewitz' *On War*.

# Notes

## Introduction

1. See Colin S. Gray, *Strategy for Chaos: Revolutions in Military Affairs and the Evidence of History* (London: Frank Cass, 2002).
2. I have examined the difficulties that beset the strategist in *The Strategy Bridge: Theory for Practice* (Oxford: Oxford University Press, 2010), ch. 4.
3. In recent decades, the leading advocate of the strategy termed 'offensive realism' has been John J. Mearsheimer at the University of Chicago. Mearsheimer's *magnum opus* is *The Tragedy of Great Power Politics*, updated edn (New York: W. W. Norton, 2014).
4. The relationship between continuity and change is a basic theme in Colin S. Gray, *Strategy and Defence Planning: Meeting the Challenge of Uncertainty* (Oxford: Oxford University Press, 2014).
5. Beatrice Heuser, 'Strategy Before the Word: Ancient Wisdom and the Modern World', *The RUSI Journal* 55/1 (February/March 2010), 36–42.
6. Thucydides, *The Landmark Thucydides: A Comprehensive Guide to 'The Peloponnesian War'*, ed. Robert B. Strassler, rev. trans. Richard Crawley (c.455–400 BC; New York: The Free Press, 1996), 43.

## 1 Politics the Master

1. Richard K. Betts, 'Should Strategic Studies Survive?' *World Politics* 50/1 (October 1997), 7–33; Richard K. Betts, 'Is Strategy an Illusion?' *International Security* 25/2 (Fall 2000), 5–50.

2. Colin S. Gray, *Strategy and Defence Planning: Meeting the Challenge of Uncertainty* (Oxford: Oxford University Press, 2014).

3. Colin S. Gray, *The Strategy Bridge: Theory for Practice* (Oxford: Oxford University Press, 2010).

4. See Beatrice Heuser, 'Strategy Before the Word: Ancient Wisdom and the Modern World', *The RUSI Journal* 55/1 (February/March 2010), 36–42.

5. For the critics, see Hew Strachan, 'Strategy in the Twenty-First Century', in Strachan and Sybille Scheipers, eds., *The Changing Character of War* (Oxford: Oxford University Press, 2011), 506. My response is explained fully in 'Conceptual "Hueys" at Thermopylae? The Challenge of Strategic Anachronism', in *The Strategy Bridge*, 267–77. Beatrice Heuser, *The Strategy Makers: Thoughts on War and Society from Machiavelli to Clausewitz* (Santa Barbara, CA: Praeger, 2010), is also highly relevant.

6. Beatrice Heuser, *The Evolution of Strategy: Thinking War from Antiquity to the Present* (Cambridge: Cambridge University Press, 2010), ch. 1.

7. Stephen Peter Rosen, *War and Human Nature* (Princeton: Princeton University Press, 2005).

8. Williamson Murray, 'Thucydides: Theorist of War', *Naval War College Review*, 66/4 (Autumn 2013), 31–46; but see also the modern academic complaints in David A. Welch, 'Why International Relations Theorists Should Stop Reading Thucydides', *Review of International Studies*, 29/3 (July 2003), 301–19.

9. Thucydides, *The Landmark Thucydides: A Comprehensive Guide to 'The Peloponnesian War'*, ed. Robert B. Strassler, rev. trans. Richard Crawley (*c*.455–400 BC; New York: The Free Press, 1996); Alan Ryan, *On Politics: A History of Political Thought from Herodotus to the Present* (London: Allen Lane, 2012).

10. Thucydides, *The Landmark Thucydides*, 43.

11. Carl von Clausewitz, *On War*, trans. Michael Howard and Peter Paret (1832–4; Princeton: Princeton University Press, 1976). Also, there is much of high value in Edward N. Luttwak, *Strategy: The Logic of War and Peace*, rev. edn (Cambridge, MA: Belknap Press of Harvard University Press, 2001).

12. For an improbable, but well-attested case, the British Expeditionary Force (BEF) was given time to escape from France in late May 1940, most probably because Hitler was becoming jealous of the success of his leading generals and wished to impose extra discipline on their obvious operational skill. See Karl-Heinz Frieser, *The Blitzkrieg Legend: The 1940 Campaign in the West* (Annapolis, MD: Naval Institute Press, 2005), chs. 7–8.

13. Thucydides tells us that King Archidamus 'had the reputation of being at once a wise and moderate man'. His arguments for prudence and caution did not prevail, but the timeless merit in his strategic views is clear indeed. Thucydides, *The Peloponnesian War*, 45–7.

14. Harold D. Lasswell, *Politics: Who Gets What, When, and How* (New York: Whittlesey House, 1936), provides the clearest argument for equating the need to study politics with the study of influence.

15. In my treatment of strategy's general theory I insist, in Dictum 2, that 'Military strategy is the direction and use made of force and the threat of force for the purposes of policy as decided by politics': Gray, *The Strategy Bridge*, 262.

16. Raymond Aron, *Peace and War: A Theory of International Relations* (New York: Doubleday, 1966), 285.

17. Nassim Nicholas Taleb, *The Black Swan: The Impact of the Highly Improbable* (New York: Random House, 2007); Gray, *Strategy and Defence Planning*.

18. For noteworthy exemplary cases, see: Barbara Tuchman, *The March of Folly: From Troy to Vietnam* (New York: Ballantine Books, 1984); Eliot A. Cohen and John Gooch, *Military Misfortunes: The Anatomy of Failure in War* (New York: Free Press, 1990); and Barry S. Strauss and Joshua Ober, *The Anatomy of Error: Ancient Military Disasters and Their Lessons for Modern Strategists* (New York: St Martin's Press, 1990).

19. Jonathan Bailey, Richard Iron and Hew Strachan, eds., *British Generals in Blair's Wars* (Farnham: Ashgate, 2013).
20. Colin S. Gray, *Perspectives on Strategy* (Oxford: Oxford University Press, 2013), ch. 2.
21. Richard F. Hamilton and Holger H. Herwig, *Decisions for War, 1914–1917* (Cambridge: Cambridge University Press, 2004), ch. 4. The most relevant section of the German Chancellor's Reichstag speech is in Michael Walzer, *Just and Unjust Wars: A Moral Argument with Historical Illustrations*, 3rd edn (New York: Basic Books, 2000), 240.
22. Gray, *The Strategy Bridge*, ch. 5.
23. Lawrence Freedman, *Strategy: A History* (Oxford: Oxford University Press, 2013), xii.
24. Clausewitz, *On War*, 177.
25. Gray, *The Strategy Bridge*, 29.
26. Heuser, *The Evolution of Strategy*, ch. 1.
27. After 1941–2 it was difficult, and eventually impossible, even for outstanding operational-level German generalship, or strategy, to make any impression on the adverse course of events. Consider the military record of Field Marshal Erich von Manstein. The story is told admirably in Mungo Melvin, *Manstein: Hitler's Greatest General* (London: Weidenfeld and Nicolson, 2010). Manstein was denied any strategic role; his demonstrated skills were limited to the battlefield. Whether or not the development of nuclear weapons provides scope for strategy remains very much a contested idea, which I treat in chapter 5 below.

## 2 Strategy: What It Is, and Why It Matters

1. The best guide by far is the reliable Beatrice Heuser. See her study *The Evolution of Strategy: Thinking War from Antiquity to the Present* (Cambridge: Cambridge University Press, 2010), ch. 1. In addition, see Lawrence Freedman, *Strategy: A History* (Oxford: Oxford University Press, 2013), especially ch. 6, and Colin S. Gray, *The Strategy Bridge: Theory for Practice* (Oxford: Oxford University Press, 2010), ch. 1.
2. See Freedman, *Strategy*, xiii.
3. I explain the important, if somewhat elusive, concept of strategic effect in *The Strategy Bridge*, ch. 5.

4. Carl von Clausewitz, *On War*, trans. Michael Howard and Peter Paret (1832–4; Princeton: Princeton University Press, 1976), 177.

5. For a very thoughtful treatment of this set of issues, see Rupert Smith, 'Epilogue', in John Andreas Olsen and Martin van Creveld, eds., *The Evolution of Operational Art: From Napoleon to the Present* (Oxford: Oxford University Press, 2011), 226–44.

6. 'War, therefore, is an act of policy', and 'war is not a mere act of policy but a true political instrument, a continuation of political activity by other means': Clausewitz, *On War*, both on p. 87.

7. See Antulio J. Echevarria II, 'Dynamic Inter-Dimensionality: A Revolution in Military Theory', *Joint Force Quarterly* 15 (Spring 1997), 36.

8. The relatively recent discovery, or invention, of an operational level of war has attracted criticism, but the idea holds good. The clearest explanation of what is meant by the concept of an operation connecting with strategy above and tactics below, is to be found in the brilliant book by Aleksandr A. Svechin, *Strategy*, 2nd edn (1927: Minneapolis: East View Information Services, 1992), 'Introduction', 67–80. A full frontal assault on the concept of an operational level of war was launched in Justin Kelly and Mike Brennan, *Alien: How Operational Art Devoured Strategy* (Carlisle, PA: Strategic Studies Institute, US Army War College, September 2009).

9. See Gray, *The Strategy Bridge*, ch. 4.

10. This is made unmistakeably clear in Mungo Melvin, *Manstein: Hitler's Greatest General* (London: Weidenfeld and Nicolson, 2010). See also Evan Mawdsley, *Thunder in the East: The Nazi–Soviet War, 1941–1945* (London: Hodder Arnold, 2005), and Jehuda L. Wallach, *The Dogma of the Battle of Annihilation: The Theories of Clausewitz and Schlieffen and Their Impact on the German Conduct of Two World Wars* (Westport, CT: Greenwood Press, 2005), chs. 16, 18.

11. Henry R. Yarger, *Strategy and the National Security Professional: Strategic Thinking and Strategy Formulation in the 21st Century* (Westport, CT: Praeger Security International, 2008), is fundamental and generally sound.

12. I explain strategy's substantially timeless general theory in the next chapter.

13. Despite its historical importance, reliable-looking studies of the reasons for success in strategy have been few and far between. Williamson Murray and Richard Hart Sinnreich, eds., *Successful Strategies: Triumphing in War and Peace from Antiquity to the Present* (Cambridge: Cambridge University Press, 2014), helps noticeably in the understanding of the more persisting reasons for success.

14. The exciting idea of the 'master strategist' preoccupies Lawrence Freedman in his *Strategy*, ch. 17. Given that he bases his analysis on a misreading of my work, I respond tersely in my book review of his study, 'Book Reviews', *International Affairs* 90/2 (March 2014).

15. See Fred Kaplan, 'The End of the Age of Petraeus: The Rise and Fall of Counterinsurgency', *Foreign Affairs* 91/1 (January/February 2013), 75–90.

16. In Afghanistan in the 2000s, NATO soldiers had to relearn the ancient strategic truth that 'There is in guerrilla warfare no such thing as a decisive battle': Mao Tse-tung, *On Guerrilla Warfare*, trans. Samuel B. Griffith (New York: Frederick A. Praeger, 1961), 52.

17. My use of the descriptor 'moral' in the text is deliberately old-fashioned, though I hope not anachronistic. It refers to character and a standard of behaviour – not primarily to some ethical audit, as is usual now. The term was widely used in my sense here until quite recently.

18. I tackle this fact in *The Strategy Bridge*, ch. 4.


## 3   Theory and Practice

1. Aleksandr A. Svechin, *Strategy*, 2nd edn (1927; Minneapolis, MIN: East View Information Services, 1992), 70.

2. Lawrence Freedman, *Strategy: A History* (Oxford: Oxford University Press, 2013), ch. 1, reminds us that chimpanzees appear to practise both politics and strategy. He is persuasive.

3. Karl Walling offers convincing reasons, mainly cultural, for why we need to be very careful not to insert our contemporary values into the debates of fifth-century-BC Greece, in

'Thucydides on Policy, Strategy, and War Termination', *Naval War College Review* 66/4 (Autumn 2013), 47–85.

4. See Beatrice Heuser, *The Evolution of Strategy: Thinking War from Antiquity to the Present* (Cambridge: Cambridge University Press, 2010), ch. 1.

5. See Colin S. Gray, *The Strategy Bridge: Theory for Practice* (Oxford: Oxford University Press, 2010), ch. 1; Gray, *Perspectives on Strategy* (Oxford: Oxford University press, 2013), ch. 1.

6. Williamson Murray, 'Thucydides: Theorist of War', *Naval War College Review*, 66/4 (autumn 2013), 42.

7. Carl von Clausewitz, *On War*, trans. Michael Howard and Peter Paret (1832–4; Princeton, NJ: Princeton University Press, 1976), 578.

8. Ibid., 141 (emphasis in the original).

9. Ibid.

10. Ibid.

11. Hew Strachan employs a helpfully wide-angled lens to consider Afghanistan in some deep historical context; see *The Direction of War: Contemporary Strategy in Historical Perspective* (Cambridge: Cambridge University Press, 2013).

12. See Tim Travers, *The Killing Ground: The British Army, the Western Front and the Emergence of Modern Warfare, 1900–1918* (London: Allen and Unwin, 1987), but see also Gary Sheffield, *The Chief: Douglas Haig and the British Army* (London: Aurum Press, 2011), for a more generous and rather more convincing view of Field-Marshal Haig's leadership in command.

13. For military context, despite the high incompetence of the Nazi regime, the Wehrmacht of the Second World War needs to be appreciated as one of the greatest fighting forces in all of strategic history. For some reasons why this was so, see Williamson Murray, *German Military Effectiveness* (Baltimore, MD: Nautical and Aviation Publishing Company of America, 1992). The finest single-authored history of the Second World War is Evan Mawdsley, *World War II: A New History* (Cambridge: Cambridge University Press, 2009).

14. See David Kilcullen, *The Accidental Guerrilla: Fighting Small Wars in the Midst of a Big One* (London: Hurst,

2009), but also Frank Ledwidge, *Losing Small Wars: British Military Failure in Iraq and Afghanistan* (New Haven, CT: Yale University Press, 2011).

15. Clausewitz states unambiguously that 'War is the realm of chance' (*On War*, 101). His cautionary words on the unpredictability of events are still not truly understood today. Both scholarly research and political documents from government make reference to a 'foreseeable future' – a contradiction in terms.

16. Borrowed gratefully from Bernard Brodie, *Strategy in the Missile Age* (Princeton, NJ: Princeton University Press, 1959), ch. 10. On assumptions, see T. X. Hammes, 'Assumptions – A Fatal Oversight', *Infinity Journal*, 1 (Winter 2010), 4–6, is prominent among the more important writings of recent years. It should never be forgotten that an assumption is a belief for which there is no evidence.

17. See Colin S. Gray, *War, Peace and International Relations: An Introduction to Strategic History*, 2nd edn (Abingdon: Routledge, 2012), ch. 19; Gray, *Perspectives on Strategy* (Oxford: Oxford University Press, 2013), ch. 3.

18. Lawrence Sondhaus, *Strategic Culture and Ways of War* (Abingdon: Routledge, 2006), offers a helpful overview of the debate about culture in strategic studies, while Patrick Porter, *Military Orientalism: Eastern War Through Western Eyes* (London: Hurst, 2009), is boldly sceptical of the recent culturalist turn in scholarship. Assessment of ideas on military culture specific to the armed services is well handled in Alastair Finlan, *Contemporary Military Culture and Strategic Studies: US and UK Armed Forces in the 21st Century* (Abingdon: Routledge, 2013). The single modest work that kick-started the debate over strategic culture was a monograph by Jack Snyder, *The Soviet Strategic Culture: Implications for Limited Nuclear Operations*, RAND R-2154-AF (Santa Monica, CA: The Rand Corporation, 1977).

19. John J. Mearsheimer, 'Why the Ukraine Crisis Is the West's Fault: The Liberal Delusions that Provoked Putin', *Foreign Affairs*, 93/5 (September/October 2014), 77–89. Mearsheimer is basically right in arguing that NATO both spoke and behaved irresponsibly in its encouragement of Ukraine to join the West.

20. Ken Booth and Nicholas J. Wheeler, *The Security Dilemma: Fear, Cooperation and Trust in World Politics* (Basingstoke: Palgrave Macmillan, 2008).

21. See Christopher Clark, *The Sleepwalkers: How Europe Went to War in 1914* (London: HarperCollins, 2012).

22. Lawrence Freedman, 'British Nuclear Targeting', in Desmond Ball and Jeffrey Richelson, eds., *Strategic Nuclear Targeting* (Ithaca, NY: Cornell University Press, 1986), 109–26.

23. Harold D. Winton, 'An Imperfect Jewel: Military Theory and the Military Profession', *The Journal of Strategic Studies*, 34/6 (December 2011), 853–77.

24. Sheffield, *The Chief*, 60.

## 4   Strategic History: Continuity and Change

1. Colin S. Gray, *War, Peace and International Relations: An Introduction to Strategic History*, 2nd edn. (Abingdon: Routledge, 2012), ch. 1.

2. See Beatrice Heuser, *The Evolution of Strategy: Thinking War from Antiquity to the Present* (Cambridge: Cambridge University Press, 2010), ch. 1; and Lawrence Freedman, *Strategy: A History* (Oxford: Oxford University Press, 2013), ch. 1.

3. Niccolò Machiavelli has been studied rather less than he deserves, as I was reminded in Antulio Echevarría II's essay on Gray, *The Strategy Bridge: Theory for Practice* (Oxford: Oxford University Press, 2010). On balance, I think Echevarría's complaint against me is correct. See his article 'Theory for Practice: But Where is Machiavelli?' *Infinity Journal*, 'The Strategy Bridge Special Edition' (March 2014), 9–11. For modern strategists, Machiavelli's most helpful book is *Discourses on Livy*, trans. and intro. Julia Conaway Bondanella and Peter Bondanella (Oxford: Oxford University Press, 1997). Other especially noteworthy studies include Sebastian de Grazia, *Machiavelli in Hell* (New York: Vintage Books, 1994); and Corrado Vivanti, *Niccolo Machiavelli: An Intellectual Biography*, trans. Simon Mac-Michael (Princeton, NJ: Princeton University Press, 2013). For a useful study that survived unscathed from the book's first edition in 1941 to its second, see Felix Gilbert,

'Machiavelli: The Renaissance of the Art of War', in Edward Mead Earle, ed., *Makers of Modern Strategy: From Machiavelli to the Nuclear Age* (Princeton, NJ: Princeton University Press, 1986), 11–31. Also, the 'Introduction' and the list of 'suggested readings' are unusually enlightening in Niccolò Machiavelli, *Art of War*, ed. and trans. Christopher Lynch (Chicago: University of Chicago Press, 2003). Other helpful studies include Quentin Skinner, *Machiavelli: A Very Short Introduction* (Oxford: Oxford University Press, 1981); and Philip Bobbitt, *The Garments of Court and Palace: Machiavelli and the World That He Made* (New York: Grove Press, 2013). The latter of these two, however, suffers from an excess of authorial opinion.

4. Readers are recommended to look carefully at the excellent essays in Victor Davis Hanson, ed., *Makers of Ancient Strategy: From the Persian Wars to the Fall of Rome* (Princeton, NJ: Princeton University Press, 2010). Ironically, perhaps, there is exceptional value for our subject in both one of the larger and one of the shorter books on war and warfare in the ancient world. See Harry Sidebottom, *Ancient Warfare: A Very Short Introduction* (Oxford: Oxford University Press, 2004), esp. ch. 5; and Adrian Goldsworthy, *Caesar: The Life of a Colossus* (London: Orion Books, 2006).

5. As usual, the Strategic Studies literature follows from the dilemmas and challenges of the day. As a brief selection of the more impressive recent studies, see Daniel Marston and Carter Malkasian, eds., *Counterinsurgency in Modern Warfare* (Botley: Osprey Publishing, 2008); David Kilcullen, *The Accidental Guerrilla* (London: Hurst, 2009); Thomas Rid and Thomas Keaney, eds., *Understanding Counterinsurgency: Doctrine, Operations and Challenges* (Abingdon: Routledge, 2010); Emile Simpson, *War from the Ground Up: Twenty-First-Century Combat as Politics* (London: Hurst, 2012); and David H. Ucko and Robert Egnell, *Counterinsurgency in Crisis: Britain and the Challenges of Modern Warfare* (New York: Colombia University Press, 2013).

6. The most persuasive historically well founded case for adaptability is advanced in Williamson Murray, *Military Adaptation in War: With Fear of Change* (Cambridge: Cambridge University Press, 2011).

7. Carl von Clausewitz, *On War*, trans. Michael Howard and Peter Paret (1832–4; Princeton, NJ: Princeton University Press, 1976), 89 (emphasis in the original).

8. I have delved into the challenging space of alleged categories of violence in my study, *Categorical Confusion? The Strategic Implications of Recognizing Challenges Either as Irregular or Traditional* (Carlisle, PA: US Army War College, Strategic Studies Institute, February 2012). Scholars are overly inclined to discover allegedly new phenomena once they have invented novel classifications for them. If one searches with sufficient diligence, it is amazing how many apparently new candidate categories appear.

9. For an outstanding recognition that the process of reciprocal violence in warfare dictates combat consequences, see Patrick Porter, *Military Orientalism: Eastern War Through Western Eyes* (London: Hurst, 2009), esp. 170.

10. Clausewitz, *On War*, 85.

11. Ibid., 75

12. See Gray, *The Strategy Bridge*, ch. 4.

13. Murray, *Military Adaptation in War*.

14. I examined carefully the quality of official and other expert futurists and was left notably unimpressed. See Colin S. Gray, *Strategy and Defence Planning: Meeting the Challenge of Uncertainty* (Oxford: Oxford University Press, 2014).

15. See Nicholas Nassim Taleb, *The Black Swan: The Impact of the Highly Improbable* (New York: Random House, 2007).

16. By the time Germany came belatedly to recognize the strengths in the Soviet system of war-making, it was too late to change course accordingly.

17. My efforts to grapple with the challenge of unknowability of the strategic future are recorded in Colin S. Gray, *Defense Planning for National Security: Navigation Aids for the Mystery Tour* (Carlisle, PA: US Army War College, Strategic Studies Institute, March 2014); Gray, *Strategy and Defence Planning*.

18. See Lawrence Freedman, *Deterrence* (Cambridge: Polity, 2004).

19. As an example of unpersuasive social scientism, it would be difficult to improve on Steven Pinker, *The Better Angels of*

*Our Nature: The Decline of Violence and its Causes* (London: Allen Lane, 2011). Christopher Coker's modest-sized book *Can War be Eliminated?* (Cambridge: Polity, 2014), provides more persuasive arguments at a fraction of the weight.

20. See Lawrence Freedman, *The Evolution of Nuclear Strategy*, 3rd edn (Basingstoke: Palgrave Macmillan, 2003); and Colin S. Gray, *War, Peace and International Relations*, ch. 15.

21. Lawrence Freedman, 'Has Strategy Reached a Dead-End?' *Futures*, 11 (April 1979), 122–31. Freedman was revisiting a furrow ploughed by Bernard Brodie in his article 'Strategy Hits a Dead End', *Harper's*, 211 (October 1955), 33–7.

22. A most emphatic 'yes' is offered in an excellent article by Williamson Murray, 'Thucydides: Theorist of War', *Naval War College Review*, 66/4 (Autumn 2013), 31–46.

23. It is prudent to keep an open mind even regarding apparently radical alternative worldviews. With that constructive thought in mind, I commend to readers' attention the distinctly non-strategic book by Ken Booth, *Theory of World Security* (Cambridge: Cambridge University Press, 2007). Booth writes his theory based on a deep personal understanding of strategy, as he demonstrated in his outstanding study, *Strategy and Ethnocentrism* (London: Croom Helm, 1979).

## 5   Strategy, Strategies and Geography

1. Colin S. Gray, 'Dowding and the British Strategy of Air Defence, 1936–1940', in Williamson Murray and Richard Hart Sinnreich, eds., *Successful Strategies: Triumphing in War and Peace from Antiquity to the Present* (Cambridge: Cambridge University Press, 2014), 241–79.

2. Carl von Clausewitz, *On War*, trans. Michael Howard and Peter Paret (1832–4; Princeton, NJ: Princeton University Press, 1976), 141.

3. Ibid.

4. The secondary title of my book *The Strategy Bridge: Theory for Practice* (Oxford: Oxford University Press, 2010) was not chosen casually.

5. Grand strategy is a seriously under-theorized but potentially dominant element in Strategic Studies. The recent Ph.D. dissertation ('Grand Strategy') by Lukas Milevski is a long-overdue comprehensive theoretical and historical examination of the idea of grand strategy (University of Reading, 2014). Also see Paul Kennedy, 'Grand Strategies and Less-than-Grand Strategies: A Twentieth-Century Critique', in Lawrence Freedman, Paul Hayes and Robert O'Neill, eds., *War, Strategy and International Politics: Essays in Honour of Sir Michael Howard* (Oxford: Clarendon Press, 1992), 228–42; John Lewis Gaddis, 'What is Grand Strategy?', lecture delivered at the conference 'American Grand Strategy after War', Triangle Institute for Security Studies and Duke University Program on American Grand Strategy, 26 February 2009, unpub.; and Charles Hill, *Grand Strategies: Literature, Statecraft, and World Order* (New Haven, CT: Yale University Press, 2010).

6. This basic question has not attracted the scholarly attention it deserves. For recent approaches to providing answers, see Harry R. Yarger, *Strategy and the National Security Professional: Strategic Thinking and Strategy Formulation in the 21st Century* (Westport, CT: Praeger Security International, 2008); Colin S. Gray, *Strategy and Defence Planning: Meeting the Challenge of Uncertainty* (Oxford: Oxford University Press, 2014); and Stephan Fruhling, *Defence Planning and Uncertainty: Preparing for the next Asia-Pacific war* (Abingdon: Routledge, 2014).

7. Kautilya, *The Arthashastra*, ed. and trans. L. N. Rangarajan (New Delhi: Penguin Books, 1992), Part X.

8. This condition of shared security concerns can be seen as the product of geopolitical anxiety, which in its turn determines geostrategic designs.

9. See Bruce W. Menning, 'War Planning and Initial Operations in the Russian Context', in Richard F. Hamilton and Holger H. Herwig, eds., *War Planning 1914* (Cambridge: Cambridge University Press, 2010), 80–142; and Paul Kennedy, ed., *War Plans of the Great Powers, 1880–1914* (London: Allen and Unwin, 1979).

10. See Gray, *Making Strategic Sense of Cyber Power: Why the Sky is Not Falling* (Carlisle, PA: Strategic Studies Institute, US Army War College, April 2013); and Jason Healey, ed.,

*A Fierce Domain: Conflict in Cyberspace, 1986–2012* (n.p.: The Cyber Conflict Association and the Atlantic Council, 2014).

11. A potent assault upon culturalism is staged in Patrick Porter, *Military Orientalism: Eastern War Through Western Eyes* (London: Hurst, 2009); for some defence of culturalism, see Colin S. Gray, *Perspectives on Strategy* (Oxford: Oxford University Press, 2013), ch. 3.

12. Holger H. Herwig, '*Geopolitik*: Haushofer, Hitler and Lebensraum', in Colin S. Gray and Geoffrey Sloan, eds., *Geopolitics, Geography and Strategy* (London: Frank Cass, 1999), 218–41.

13. See Aaron L. Friedberg, *Beyond Air–Sea Battle: The Debate Over US Military Strategy in Asia* (Abingdon: Routledge for the International Institute for Strategic Studies, 2014), esp. 11.

14. See Halford J. Mackinder, *Democratic Ideals and Reality* (1919; New York, W. W. Norton, 1962); and Nicholas J. Spykman, *America's Strategy in World Politics: The United States and the Balance of Power* (1942; New Brunswick, NJ: Transaction Publishers, 2007); Spykman, *The Geography of the Peace* (1944; Hamden: Archon Books, 1969).

15. Mackinder, *Democratic Ideals and Reality*, 150.

16. Geoffrey Parker, *Mackinder: Geography as an Aid to Statecraft* (Oxford: Clarendon Press, 1982); and Brian W. Blouet, *Halford Mackinder: A Biography* (College Station: Texas A&M University Press, 1987).

17. Spykman, *The Geography of the Peace*, 43. Analyses of Spykman's geopolitical theory are all too rare, but for two lonely exceptions see David Wilkinson, 'Spykman and Geopolitics', in Ciro E. Zoppo and Charles Zorgbibe, eds., *On Geopolitics: Classical and Nuclear* (Dordrecht: Martinus Nijhoff Publishers, 1985), 77–129; and Colin S. Gray, 'Nicholas John Spykman, the Balance of Power and International Order', *Journal of Strategic Studies* (forthcoming).

18. It is gratifying to note that Spykman's ideas have been somewhat revived recently in Robert D. Kaplan, *The Revenge of Geography* (New York: Random House, 2012), esp. ch. 6.

19. Horace Walpole, quoted in Brendan Simms, *Europe: The Struggle for Supremacy, 1453 to the Present* (London: Allen Lane, 2013), 95.

20. See Gray, *Making Strategic Sense of Cyber Power*.
21. 'For after all allowances have been made for historical differences, wars still resemble each other more than they resemble any other human activity': Michael Howard, *The Causes of Wars and Other Essays* (London: Counterpoint, 1983), 214.
22. Probably the finest brief explanation of military service cultures is that provided in J. C. Wylie, *Military Strategy: A General Theory of Power Control* (1967; Annapolis, MD: Naval Institute Press, 1989). For particular foci, see Roger W. Barnett, *Navy Strategic Culture: Why the Navy Thinks Differently* (Annapolis, MD: Naval Institute Press, 2009); Brian McAllister Linn, *The Echo of Battle: The Army's Way of War* (Cambridge, MA: Harvard University Press, 2007); and Colin S. Gray, *Airpower for Strategic Effect* (Maxwell AFB, AL: Air University Press, 2012), ch. 3.

## 6  Strategy and the Future

1. Christopher Coker, *Can War be Eliminated?* (Cambridge: Polity, 2014)
2. See Colin S. Gray, 'Why Strategy is Difficult', in Thomas G. Mahnken and Joseph A Maiolo, eds., *Strategic Studies: A Reader* (Abingdon: Routledge, 2008), 391–7; and Gray, *The Strategy Bridge: Theory for Practice* (Oxford: Oxford University Press, 2010), ch. 4.
3. Richard Rhodes, *The Making of the Atomic Bomb* (New York: Touchstone Books, 1986), Gerard J. DeGroot, *The Bomb: A Life* (London: Jonathan Cape, 2004) and Jeremy Bernstein, *Nuclear Weapons: What You Need to Know* (Cambridge: Cambridge University Press, 2008) are particularly informative.
4. As slightly bizarre education or even entertainment, one should read and consider Herman Kahn, *On Escalation: Metaphors and Scenarios* (New York: Praeger, 1965).
5. I explained my scepticism at length in C. S. Gray, *House of Cards: Why Arms Control Must Fail* (Ithaca, NY: Cornell University Press, 1992). The history of arms control from 1992 to 2014 does not incline me towards revision of my strongly negative view of the practical value of the enterprise.

6. Scholars are not always pleased to be told that the absence of a happening is not evidence at all. In other words, no evidence means nothing regarding causation. Obviously, this glittering insight is a little embarrassing for those strategists who like to believe that their favoured schemes caused deterrence to work. In reality, we do not know what, if anything, causes peace. For insightful probing of this matter of negative evidence, see Nassim Nicholas Taleb, *The Black Swan: The Impact of the Highly Improbable* (New York: Random House, 2010).

7. See Lawrence Freedman, *The Evolution of Nuclear Strategy*, 3rd edn (Basingstoke: Palgrave Macmillan, 2003); and Michael Quinlan, *Thinking About Nuclear Weapons: Principles, Problems, Prospects* (Oxford: Oxford University Press, 2009).

8. For a particularly apposite commentary on the theory that reductions in the number of nuclear weapons would be beneficial for international order, see Keith B. Payne (Study Director), *Minimum Deterrence: Examining the Evidence* (Fairfax, VA: National Institute Press, 2013).

## Conclusion: What Do We Know with High Confidence?

1. Colin S. Gray, *Strategy and Defence Planning: Meeting the Challenge of Uncertainty* (Oxford: Oxford University Press, 2014).

2. I have advanced and explained this argument in Gray, *Modern Strategy* (Oxford: Oxford University Press, 1999), chs. 11–12.

3. Superior studies of strategy are in short supply. However, two recent additions to their slim ranks merit attention. These are Thomas M. Kane, *Strategy: Key Thinkers: A Critical Engagement* (Cambridge: Polity, 2013); and Williamson Murray and Richard Hart Sinnreich, eds., *Successful Strategies: Triumphing in War and Peace from Antiquity to the Present* (Cambridge: Cambridge University Press, 2014).

4. I argue and explain this claim in Gray, *Strategy and Defence Planning*.

5. See the classic study by Richard E. Neustadt and Ernest R. May, *Thinking in Time: The Uses of History for Decision-Makers* (New York: Free Press, 1986), esp. ch. 14.

6. Karl Marx's pejorative words were that 'the tradition of all the dead generations weighs like a nightmare on the brains of the living': Marx, *The Eighteenth Brumaire of Louis Napoleon* [1852], in Marx and Friedrich Engels, *Selected Works in Two Volumes*, Vol. I (Moscow: Foreign Languages Publishing House, 1962), 247.

# Index